WITH A
BIBLE
IN THEIR
HANDS

WITH A BIBLE IN THEIR HANDS

BAPTIST PREACHING IN THE SOUTH 1679-1979

Al Fasol

BROADMAN
&HOLMAN
PUBLISHERS

Nashville, Tennessee

4210-89
0-8054-1089-9

Dewey Decimal Classification: 286
Subject Heading: SOUTHERN BAPTISTS // HISTORY
Library of Congress Card Catalog Number: 93-7351
Printed in the United States of America

Unless otherwise stated, all Scripture quotations are from the *King James Version* of the Bible

Library of Congress Cataloging-in-Pulbication Data

Fasol, Al.

    With a Bible in their hands: three centuries of Baptist preaching in the South / Al Fasol.
      p. cm.
    Includes bibliographical reference and index.
    ISBN 0-8054-1089-9
    1. Preaching—United States —History. 2. Southern Baptist Convention—Sermons—History and criticism. 3. Baptists —Sermons—History and criticism.
    I. Title.

BV4208.U6F37   1994
251'.008'261—dc20   93-7351
                                                    CIP

This history is dedicated to

Hubert and Freida Fox,
Royalton Baptist Church, Royalton, Illinois,
Pennington Baptist Church, Pennington, Texas, and
Powderly Baptist Church, Powderly, Texas—

each of whom invested so much in my future.

Table of Contents

Preface

In the late 1950s, Dr. H.C. Brown, Jr., who taught preaching at Southwestern Baptist Theological Seminary from 1949 until his death in 1973, dreamed of writing a history of Southern Baptist preaching. Brown supervised several doctoral dissertations on the subject and was keenly interested in writing the book. I had first experienced the passing of his mantle in 1972. (In no way would I claim to have taken his place; I assumed his teaching schedule.) H.C. knew there was a strong possibility that he would not survive his second heart surgery in the spring of 1973. He said to my wife and me, "I have a dream that Al will soon teach preaching at Southwestern." He paused for a long time and then said, "I also dream that you will be my colleague, but if not, I pass my mantle to you. I know you will wear it well." In 1990, after completing some other writing projects, I felt again that H.C. was passing his mantle on to me. This time it was to fulfill his dream of a book that surveys the history of Southern Baptist preaching.

In the summer of 1990, I read the other dissertations (I had written one myself) that H.C. had supervised on the history of Southern Baptist preaching. These dissertations saved me many hours. The resource material I would need was carefully compiled and documented as it should be in a doctoral dissertation. I did choose to read these resource materials for myself. I was not at all concerned with whether the other dissertations used this material accurately. I was entirely confident that they did. I thought it paramount that I study the resources to "feel" what those early authors and preachers intended us to feel when they wrote and preached. I am indebted, therefore, to Cecil Sherman, Farrar Patterson, Edmund Lacy, and Lavonn Brown for pointing to the diaries, books, tapes, and other materials I needed for this book.

The time periods in the book were divided in relation to Baptist history whenever that was possible. We know that Baptists arrived in South Carolina in the 1670s. The first time period covers the 1670s to 1800. The year 1800 was chosen for convenience and because I wanted to concentrate, in a separate chapter, on the years leading up to the birth of the Southern Baptist Convention. Therefore, chapter 1 covers the late 1670s to 1800, and chapter 2 1800-1845. Chapter 3 surveys the years 1845-1900. Again, the year 1900 was chosen for convenience, but also because Southern Baptists were in a transition period in 1900. As the nineteenth century closed, Southern Baptists were moving away from one doctrinal controversy and were also gearing up for another. Chapter 4 reviews preaching in the years 1900-1945; the closing date was chosen because that was the end of World War II, and George W. Truett died in July 1944. By 1945 Southern Baptists were moving into a distinctly new era. Chapter 5 covers 1945-1979. The later date was chosen for two reasons. Obviously, the Southern Baptist Convention's most recent controversy began in 1979. Many changes in Southern Baptist life began then and continue to this date. I am much too close to these changes at this time to write objectively about them. The second reason for this date is that 1979 rounds out three hundred years of Baptist and Southern Baptist preaching. Three hundred years is a good round figure in which to close this brief study.

In addition to the authors of the doctoral dissertations already mentioned, I am indebted deeply to many others. Jess Northcutt and Leon McBeth offered many helpful suggestions and corrections. Ed Floyd and James and Jean Preveaux graciously provided hospitality and transportation so I could check historical sites and writings in and around South Carolina. The library staff at Furman University was kind and helpful. Their willingness to copy and transmit many documents saved me much time and money. Vicki Barrs and Kathy Mishler typed and retyped the manuscript. To each of these people I offer my gratitude.

Introduction

Our Baptist ancestors took preaching seriously, and for good reason. Preaching benefited them in a number of ways. Foremost, of course, preaching confronted them with a message from God's holy Word by means of a God-appointed messenger. God knew from the beginning of time that His people would be vulnerable to superstition and attracted to mystical and mysterious practices that purported to have secret and "divine" sanction. In Deuteronomy 18:9-12, Moses warned the people:

> When thou art come into the land which the Lord thy God giveth thee, thou shalt not learn to do after the abominations of those nations.
>
> There shall not be found among you any one that maketh his son or his daughter to pass through the fire, or that useth divination, or an observer of times, or an enchanter, or a witch, or a charmer, or a consulter with familiar spirits, or a wizard, or a necromancer.
>
> For all that do these things are an abomination unto the Lord.

Instead, in Deuteronomy 18:18-20, God said that He would provide a preacher to communicate His words:

> I will raise them up a Prophet from among their brethren, like unto thee, and will put my words in his mouth; and he shall speak unto them all that I shall command him.
>
> And it shall come to pass, that whosoever will not hearken unto my words which he shall speak in my name, I will require it of him. But the prophet, which shall presume to speak a word in my name, which I have not commanded him to speak, or that shall speak in the name of other gods, even that prophet shall die.

Further, God explained how the people could know when a preacher was speaking God's word or not (Deut. 18:22):

> When a prophet speaketh in the name of the Lord, if the thing
> follow not, nor come to pass, that is the thing which the Lord hath
> not spoken, but the prophet hath spoken it presumptuously: thou
> shalt not be afraid of him.

That preaching is to be based on the Word of God is again emphasized in Nehemiah 8:8:

> So they read in the book in the law of God distinctly, and gave
> the sense, and caused them to understand the reading.

Instead of being misused by mystical, authoritarian, somehow convincing would-be messengers from God, preaching is to be based on God's Word and communicated by God's messenger so that God's people will be confronted with His Word. This is a good reason for taking preaching seriously.

Our Baptist ancestors found that preaching enriched them intellectually as well as spiritually. Theology was as important to them as business and entertainment have become to us. As a result, the sermon became a time for active mental participation. The preacher read from the Bible, and the people anticipated what would follow. If the sermon was doctrinal, for example, they wanted to hear how the Bible supported the preacher's doctrinal stance.

Children learned to sharpen their reasoning powers by listening to sermons. Families customarily discussed the week's sermons (usually two on Sunday and one on Thursday) by calling on the children to recite the major points of the sermon, then to suggest how these salient points related to their daily lives, and finally to offer some pertinent personal comments. These exercises in listening perceptively, developing their memories, organizing their thoughts in a clear and logical manner, and communicating these thoughts orally were of tremendous benefit in the mental growth of our ancestors. Thus, the sermon was used primarily to receive a message from God, but it was also utilized as a classroom experience in applied thinking.

The sermon also served much the same purpose as the editorial section of a newspaper. Often the preacher was the most educated (and frequently the only formally educated) person in the community. The sermon, therefore, became the primary means of interpreting and understanding current events. Through the sermon, the people learned of their duties as children of God and as citizens. Preaching was their guide for eternal life and ethical fulfillment of their daily lives.

Physical discomfort certainly worked against attentiveness, which characterized churchgoers in colonial America. Early church buildings had no artificial lighting or any means for cooling or heating. Pews were straight-backed and hard. Physical comforts such as cushions or heated bricks to warm the feet in the winter were considered signs of spiritual softness. The increase of physical comfort was thought to decrease spiritual well-being and mental alertness.

Despite the discomfort, the maximum length of sermons ranged from two to four hours. Members of the congregation went to church expecting to be physically uncomfortable but spiritually and mentally blessed. Under conditions that would try the dedication of an ancient Spartan, preachers commanded attention and left the people hungry for more. How did they do that?

- The early colonists expressed much of their dissent through the church. Dissent always requires careful reasoning, and careful reasoning must be done in lengthy discourses. The people demanded the preaching of long sermons that established the intellectual base for all of their beliefs, especially their dissent.

- The sermon was the best means for intellectual exercise. For our ancestors, intellectual exercise was a necessity, not a luxury. Survival in those days meant more than toilsome labor. Initiative, creativity, and good planning also were required for the development of tools and improvement of crops, among other things, which were directly related to the ability to survive in the colonies. A brief sermon simply would not have challenged the minds of our forefathers.

- The sermons appealed to them emotionally. Our Baptist ancestors found some healthy emotional release when preachers spoke with vivid and sensational descriptions of theological and even mundane daily events. For example, although it is unfair to judge his preaching on the basis of one sermon, Jonathan Edwards'

"Sinners in the Hands of an Angry God" is the archetype of early American preaching: confronting people with the Bible in an intellectually stimulating and challenging way, and with vivid, sensational description.

- Preachers paced their heavy monologues by adding occasional "homely" illustrations. (*Homely* is a word used by Benjamin Franklin to describe the illustrative material of his favorite preachers.) These homely illustrations provided some analogy from everyday experience and related that experience to the sermon. One common illustration of our colonial era related the resurrection (1 Cor. 15) to an onion. The earthly layers are peeled away until we come to the soul that is the core of our being.

- Preaching provided a wholesome diversion from the daily routines that were largely geared toward survival.

- Preachers spoke in a plain, simple style. They spoke in the language of the people without necessarily sacrificing profound thinking.

PREAChiNq iN tHE SouTh

Preaching in the South took on a deeper eloquence, traditionally, than preaching in the North. Speculation as to why this was so generally centers on climatic and cultural differences. Warmer climates seemed to dictate a slower pace of life. This slower pace allowed more time for meditation, especially for meditation on things of beauty. Things of beauty should be described in beautiful (that is, eloquent) ways; thus, the bent toward eloquence in preaching in the South.

W.J. Cash asserts that this eloquence resulted from rationalizations that sought to justify slavery. Cash claims these rationalizations brought on a "remarkable tendency to seize on lovely words . . . to heap them in redundant profusion one upon another . . . until there is nothing left but . . . the ploy of primitive rhythm on the secret springs of emotion."[1]

1. W.J. Cash, *The Mind of the South* (New York: Doubleday, 1954), see 63, 90. For a more balanced view of the history of eloquence in the South, see W.W. Braden, "Southern Oratory Reconsidered: A Search for an Image," *Southern Speech Journal,* xxix (Summer 1964), 303-315.

Whatever its source and its raison d'étre, eloquence in preaching did abound in the South. We will have opportunity to read many eloquent sermonic phrases in the pages to come.

How the Role of Preaching Has Changed

Obviously the role of preaching has changed from the days of our earliest Baptist ancestors to the present day. Three major reasons for this change follow:

First, the need for dissent waned. Certainly there was and continues to be both inter- and intradenominational dissent. These differences were limited, however, to specific regions or specific groups, and they concerned doctrine rather than freedom. The American psyche was not totally involved in these later dissents. Localized dissents do not inspire as much passion as a dissent that is more widely felt.

Second, as the public school system grew and eventually became mandatory, the pulpit ceased to be *the* highest intellectual resource for most Americans. McGuffey's *Reader* took the place of the Bible for people learning to read. The public (and parochial) classroom became the center for integrating, memorizing, and applying information.

Southern Baptists have had ambivalent feelings about formal education, and these inconsistencies need to be noted here so that we might better understand our shifting attitudes toward preaching. Early in the development of our school systems, Southern Baptists seemed to be pro-formal education but suspicious of knowledge. Southern Baptists, it seems, wanted formal educational opportunities, but they also wanted to be certain that "book learnin" did not take the place of practical experience. While most Southern Baptists agreed (and agree) with this philosophy, there were, and are, some who evidently feel that ignorance is knowledge and knowledge is evil. This attitude has been especially persistent among some people with relation to theological education. These attitudes, as we will see, affected many of our earlier preachers.

Third, preaching is not the *only* wholesome diversion available to us. In fact, a church is no longer the only source of wholesome diversion. Churches have long recognized this. Many churches, rural and urban, have built Christian life centers for recreation and other activities, expanding their ministries to meet the needs and changing interests in the communities they serve. The problem of diversion, however, is more complex than that. Many less than wholesome diversions are available today, and they are increasing daily. Their increase reflects their popularity even among the members of our churches. This very thorny issue has had significant impact on worship in general and on preaching in particular. An increased demand for worship and preaching to be less formal and more relaxed, even entertaining, has brought changes in our thinking about worship and preaching.

WhAT ElEMENTS of PREAChiNG CONTiNUE

Despite the differences, some elements of preaching remain the same. Many preachers still use vivid and sensational descriptions. Also, illustrations, homely or otherwise, are still important to preaching. Recent communication studies show that communication that includes an analogy is much more persuasive than communication that is restricted to only a statement of relevant facts. Analogies are not the only form of illustration for preaching; but regardless of the type, illustrations continue to play a significant role in preaching.

The need for plain, simple language remains a priority for preaching. Jesus set the standard for us in the use of language. No one communicated more profoundly in simple language than He did, and we would do well to follow His example. Every preacher should read the sayings of Jesus at least twice a year to appreciate the beauty of the simple words that shaped His thoughts. Even though the disciples needed help in finding the meaning of some of the parables, Jesus usually was immediately understood. When He said, "Render unto Caesar what is Caesar's, and render unto God what is God's," every listener heard a deep, abiding truth in plain, simple language. Good preaching does the same thing.

Why This Book Was Written

The purpose of this book is to examine how preaching has been done in many different ways by many different people in the life of Southern Baptists. Chapter 1 (1679-1800) reviews the deepest roots of Baptist preaching in the South. We start with William Screven, but only after acknowledging that there was Baptist worship in Charleston for several years before he arrived. Chapter 2 (1800-1845) examines the preachers who were the immediate movers and shakers for the founding of the Southern Baptist Convention in 1845. Chapter 3 (1845-1900) looks at the preachers and statesmen who put the Southern Baptist Convention on ecclesiological maps. Chapter 4 (1900-1945) covers the gradual transition from the formal oratorical style of preaching to what would become a more informal conversational style especially after 1945. Chapter 5 (1945-1979) takes a look at the last of the oratorical preachers and the first of the preachers who combined the oratorical and conversational styles. The 1979 ending date rounds the time period off to three hundred years of Baptist/Southern Baptist Convention preaching.

Each chapter begins with a brief review of the times and the theological climate. Representative sermons are briefly analyzed and synopses or excerpts are offered to give us a taste of the preaching of our forefathers. Renowned and renounced preachers are included. Most of them were colorful, some were pedantic, but all of them were committed. I am frequently asked, "What one quality stands out in all great preachers?" Some had eloquence, but not all of them. Some had forceful personalities, but not all of them. Some were gregarious and loquacious, but not all of them. Some were daring and adventuresome, but not all of them. Some were humble, but not all of them. The one feature that stands out is their willingness to work hard. They worked to know, understand, appreciate, and communicate scriptural truth. They worked hard to prayerfully understand God and His divine will for their lives. They worked hard, even passionately, to help Christians grow. They prioritized hard work in reaching people for Christ.

Preachers Selected for This Book

Various criteria were used for selecting preachers to be included in this book. The first obvious criterion was availability of sermons. This criterion stipulated that primary resource material existed and could be used to analyze and evaluate some preachers and their preaching. The mere fact that a preacher's sermons had been published, however, was insufficient reason for including him in this study.

A second criterion centered on the life and contributions of an individual preacher. Most of the men included in this book stood out for their positive Baptist life and preaching. A few more names were added after they were discovered by scouring state Baptist newspapers, journals, and history books to find clues that might point to an able but unrenowned preacher. Some who are remembered for their negative input on Baptist life are included because, in some ways and at various times, they were effective preachers.

The third criterion centered on the testimony of other preachers and congregations about the preaching of particular men. When several people affirm the preaching of a particular man, we can assume that some effective preaching was being done.

Finally, homiletical criteria were applied. Did the sermons of an individual preacher exemplify a strong relationship between the sermon and the text? This criterion was important to this study. The centrality of Scripture in the sermon is vital in any study such as this. Some of the sermons were considered to have direct biblical authority. That is, the sermon obviously proclaimed that which the biblical text taught. Some sermons were considered to have secondary biblical authority. That is, the sermon picked up a strong but not the central idea of the biblical text. Some sermons were considered to have only a casual biblical authority. That is, the sermon developed only a minor idea in the biblical text.

How did the preacher functionally develop his sermon? Did he use explanation of the text so as to feed directly the congregation from the Bible? If so, did the preacher adequately explain the text, or did he overuse explanation to the point of becoming esoteric and irrelevant? Did the preacher use application? Was the application directed to his congregation? A key question was asked here; that is, did the application build a bridge from the Bible to the lives of the congregation? Was the application vital and essential to the congregation or was it mundane and trite? Effective preaching should be based on the Bible, but it should also have a lively relationship to the congregation. Did the illustrations contribute to the general flow of the sermon and to the understanding of the text or were they used to sensationalize the sermon or to cover up for the lack of explanation? Did the preacher use argumentation to persuade the congregation to change an attitude or action? If so, was the argumentation compelling, logical, and convincing, or was the argument built on the weak and overused straw-man approach?

Are the preachers included in this book the greatest preachers in history of the Southern Baptist Convention? Actually, I'm not at all certain that the terminology "great preachers" is appropriate. What makes one preacher great and another, albeit an effective preacher, not great? Undoubtedly, a host of preachers did great work for the Lord, but their names were not available to be included in this book.

The purpose of this book is to examine from historical, theological, homiletical, and communicational perspectives the many different ways by many different people in the life of Southern Baptists that preaching has been done. This critical study should provide us a better perspective as to what preaching was, what preaching is, and what preachers are becoming in Southern Baptist life.

CHAPTER 1

ARRIVING IN THE SOUTH
(1679-1800)

Baptists from England and Huguenots from France eagerly sailed to the southern colony known vaguely to them only as "Carolina." The coast of South Carolina must have looked promising to those immigrants, particularly to the Bullens, a Baptist family from England, as they sailed into Charleston harbor in the late 1670s. It was then known as Charles Town. Nearly ten thousand people lived in the Charleston harbor area. The nearby forests of ash, pine, myrtle, cedar, and magnolia abounded in lush growth. Deer, rabbits, wild turkey, and partridges lived in the forest and were available to all hunters. Fish and oysters were especially plentiful in the harbor and up and down the coast.

Changes in the old settlement occurred steadily. Charles Town was soon to become old Charles Town. The streets, shops, and homes that would be the new Charles Town, already under construction when the Bullens arrived, were settled in 1680.

The Bullens found everything they had hoped for. America offered a place to live pleasantly and a place to worship freely. They especially appreciated a place to worship freely. After suffering religious persecution in their native countries, these Baptists envisioned a better day in South Carolina. There was no Baptist church in Charles Town when the Bullens arrived, but that was destined to change soon. The Bullens and the other immigrants like them had brought the beginnings of Baptist work to the southern colonies.

The Bullens (variously spelled Bullen, Bulline, Bullein, and Bulling in South Carolina legal records) and other Baptist families who had either accompanied them or arrived in Charles Town soon after, had an ordered set of priorities. As soon as they could, they filed for land warrants (titles) in or near Charles Town. They knew from their experiences in England that landowners, often referred to as "very respected citizens," exercised near monopolistic control of Parliament and therefore English law. They were determined to be landowners in South Carolina—not in order to become aristocrats, but instead to become "very respected citizens" whose voices would be heard in matters of law, especially as it related to religious liberty. In line with this goal, public records show that between 1684 and 1702 John Raven, a Baptist, secured five land warrants. In the 1680s, other Baptists—Richard Baker, Jonathan Barker, Benjamin Blake, and Thomas Cates—applied for and were granted land warrants.

For a few years, this small group of Baptists in the South held their services at the home of William Chapman. They were steady in their commitment, but small in number. Small, that is, until the church nearly doubled in size in 1696 when the Rev. William Screven and twenty-five to thirty members of the Baptist church in Kittery, Maine, moved to Charles Town. These new members were in the shipbuilding business. The timber around Kittery was scarce. Access to timber away from Kittery was perilous because of hostile Indians. Screven and the other church members needed a new location to pursue their trade. He was probably aware of the Baptist group in Charles Town, and undoubtedly knew that the heavily wooded coastal South Carolina was a major trading area. That made it a prime site for shipbuilders. Possibly with the encouragement of the Charles Town Baptists, Screven and several members of the Kittery church made the move. Since the Kittery fellowship arrived in Charles Town as a formal church body, historically, the First Baptist Church of

Charles Town dates its beginning to the constitution of the Kittery Church in 1682.

The dream of a church building was fulfilled on July 18, 1699, when William Elliott transferred "Lot No. 62 on Church Street in Charles Town" as a gift to the Baptist church of which he was a member. By 1700 the Baptist meeting house was constructed. Thus, Baptists had firmly established themselves in the South as "very respected citizens" who were serious in their commitment to freedom of religious expression.

The modest beginnings of Baptists in the South in the seventeenth century were not indicative of how Baptists would increase in number and influence in the eighteenth century. Baptist growth was triggered by the First Great Awakening which began around 1740. This widespread revival led to an increase in the number of Baptists, and it guided Baptists toward a sense of unity. After these early Baptist roots were established, many theological, sociological, and political controversies began to dominate Baptist preaching, The most significant theological controversy involved predestination. Baptists were divided into Particular (Calvinistic) and General (Arminian) groups. This controversy began in England, but in America, especially under the influence of theologian Andrew Fuller after 1785, the Particular Baptists moderated their stance. As a result, Particular and General Baptists in America eventually began to cooperate in missionary and evangelistic efforts.

Controversy Among Baptists

While the First Great Awakening brought some unity to Baptists, it also hastened the beginning of a new controversy. New labels arose for differing Baptists. Regular Baptists (those who held to a "dignified" worship practice) shied away from the emotionalism of the revival meeting. Separate Baptists (who preferred more emotional, less structured worship practice) saw the revivals as divinely endorsed, and so "separated" themselves from what they considered the cold formalism of Regular Baptist churches. Regular and Separate Baptists in the South were more distinctly divided than were their brothers and sisters in New England.

The rift between Regular and Separate Baptists had sociological as well as theological dimensions, and both affected preaching. The primary theological concern was soteriology. Conversion was of immense importance to the Separate Baptist. Evangelistic preaching was emphasized to the point of neglecting to preach for the growth of those who were already saved. However, toward the end of the century, Regular Baptists had to admit that they had preached for the edification of saints to the point that they were negligent about evangelism. Regular Baptist pastors were alarmed to find that their congregations increasingly included some members who had been baptized but not converted and some who were converted after they were baptized. With both sides willing to admit their mistakes, pastors such as Richard Furman were human arcs that eventually welded Regular and Separate Baptists in the South. Their dispute was never totally resolved, but they did work, fellowship, and cooperate with some mutual respect.

The sociological issue, which was closely akin to the theological issue, had to do primarily with education, or more specifically, the lack of it. The majority of Regular Baptists believed in education of ministers. Separate Baptists were more concerned with what they called the "immediacy of the Spirit" in their preaching. To a Separate Baptist, formal theological education and advance preparation of sermons were an inferior replacement for what the Holy Spirit prompted them to say as they preached. Without some training, however, their sermons were shallow and repetitious. It took the irenic spirit of men like David Thomas to help Separates be less suspicious of education. To this day that part of the Separate legacy is still found in Baptist life in the South.

Another controversy arose in the 1740s when Regular Baptists accepted the Philadelphia Confession of Faith. This Confession was quickly endorsed by Regular Baptists and had a direct impact in the South for more than a century. Separate Baptists, suspicious of the carefully worded document, at first declared that they would have no creed but the Bible. Eventually, the Separate Baptists accepted the Confession with reservations. By the end of the century the influence of the Confession in Separate Baptist sermons was apparent.

Compensation for the pastor was not a major controversy, but was a brief problem for Baptists. Note the insight it provides into the Baptist ways of thinking. At first Baptists in general, including most preachers, stood adamantly against "paying the parson." This early stance against a salary for a pastor was not a hermeneutical issue. Instead it was largely a stance against Anglicanism. Baptists did not want to be tainted by any apparent association with Anglican ways. The Anglican church represented many things Baptists abhorred, especially its relation to the state. At this time the state paid the salary of the Anglican pastor. The money was usually derived from taxes. Obviously, this was as odious as it could be to a Baptist. Anglican pastors were described as cold, formal in their preaching, uncaring for the spiritual welfare of the people, but much concerned about the material welfare of the clergy. One of the roots of this cold formality, as Baptists saw it, was the practice of receiving a salary, especially since the salary was provided by the government. Anglican ministers believed that compensation was necessary in order for them to focus their efforts on preaching and other ministerial duties, rather than "farming or something" which would rob them of time to do God's work.

John Leland, a virulent anti-compensation Virginia Baptist preacher, once debated an Anglican minister who believed that ministers needed state support to compensate them for the time they spent preparing their sermons. James Ireland recounted the incident this way:

> Leland answered that he could expound the Scriptures without special preparation, and the Anglican challenged him to preach on a text to be provided just before beginning the sermon. Leland accepted the challenge. Leland went into the pulpit of the Anglican the following Sunday. As he ascended to the pulpit he was handed a text which proved to be Numbers 22:21, "And Balaam saddled his ass." "Mr. Leland first commented on the account from which the text was taken, and then said he should divide his subject into three

parts: 1st, Balaam, as a false prophet, represents a hireling clergy; 2d, the saddle represents their enormous salaries; the 3d, the dumb ass represents the people who will bear such a load." This was a theme he could develop with no difficulty whatever.[1]

Leland's sermon did nothing to help the cause of biblical authority in preaching, but it is representative of Baptist attitudes about Anglicanism as well as about salaries for pastors.

By the end of the eighteenth century, David Thomas, Richard Furman, and others were able to help change this attitude, and a salary for a pastor became increasingly acceptable.

Freedom from the tyranny of England was a common theme in Baptist preaching. Baptist preachers who supported the Revolution were much more prevalent than those who did not. Particular, General, Regular, or Separate, Baptists in the South, often at their own peril, preached in favor of eradicating British control. Oliver Hart, for example, fled Charleston in 1780 just ahead of the British troops who surely would have arrested him. Edmund Botsford lost title to his property in England because he not only preached in favor of the Revolution, but also served as a chaplain for the United States Army.

After the Revolutionary War, Baptists continued to insist on personal freedom, including freedom of religion. John Leland was the chief spokesman for Baptists (and perhaps everyone with similar concerns) in the South. Leland eventually had an important conversation with James Madison, who had strong Baptist support in Virginia and was that state's representative to the Constitutional Convention. Tradition tells us that Leland, the leader of the General Committee of Virginia, pressured Madison into taking a strong stance on religious liberty and other rights. The tradition has never been fully verified. In light of Leland's views of strong Baptist backing, and of Madison's stance at the Constitutional Convention, the tradition has not been largely rejected either.

Slavery and abolitionism also affected preaching in this period of American history. Leland, who supported religious liberty

---

1. James Ireland, *The Life of the Rev. James Ireland* (Winchester, Va.: J. Foster, 1819), 125.

for non-Christians as well as Christians, was also one of the first Baptist preachers in America to speak against slavery. Characteristically, Leland, a maverick in many ways and strongly for freedom in every way, was an abolitionist in Virginia, the very state where slavery was instituted in America in 1619.

Later, Richard Furman took the opposite position and used all of his considerable intellectual abilities to give theological justification for slavery. While calling for kind treatment of slaves by their masters (as taught in the Bible), Furman was ever for keeping the slaves in their "place." In a letter to the Governor of South Carolina, dated December 24, 1822, Furman reported:

> very respectable Citizens have been averse to the proposal under consideration; the proposal for appointing a Day of Public Thanksgiving for our preservation from the intended Insurrection (of the slave population), on account of the influence it might be supposed to have on the Black Population — by giving publicity to the subject in *their view,* and by affording them excitements to attempt something further of the same nature.[2]

This brief glimpse of the times sets the stage for the introduction of many of the main preachers. Our study centers on Regular Baptists. Separate Baptists, given as they were to the "immediacy of the Spirit," left only a small amount of material for us to study. As already indicated, the story of Baptist preaching in the South begins with William Screven.

William Screven (1629-1713)

William Screven's first step from obscurity into history occurred when he was arrested for speaking against infant baptism in Kittery, Maine, in late 1682. In order to avoid continued conflict with civic and ecclesiastical authorities in Maine, and because his shipbuilding business could no longer be supported there, Screven, along with several other Baptists, moved to South Carolina. Thus, Screven became the first Baptist pastor (and perhaps preacher) in the South.

---

2. Richard Furman, *Exposition of the Views of Baptists Relative to the Coloured Population of the United States,* Reprinted in *Richard Furman: Life and Legacy* by James A. Rogers (Macon, Ga: Mercer University Press, 1985), 275.

Screven was born in Somerton, England. He moved to Massachusetts in 1668. Records show that Screven purchased property in Kittery, Maine, November 15, 1673. Kittery had a navigable harbor, but could not compete commercially with Boston. Eventually, the harbor at Kittery was used for shipbuilding. He joined the First Baptist Church of Boston June 21, 1681. The Boston church licensed Screven to preach on January 11, 1682, and ordained him on September 25, 1682. His preaching against infant baptism and his refusal to attend the public meetinghouse as prescribed by colonial law led to his arrest and his decision to relocate the Kittery congregation to South Carolina.

The church which was born in Kittery in 1682 is still alive as First Baptist Church, Charleston, South Carolina.

At age 70, Screven announced his retirement. The closing paragraph of Screven's parting sermon was recorded by an early biographer named James Wesberry. This is the only portion of any sermon preached by Screven available to us. Notice the depth of pastoral concern.

> And now, for a close of all, my dear brethren and sisters (whom God hath made me, poor unworthy me, instrument of gathering and settling in the faith and order of the gospel), my request is that you as speedily as possible supply yourself with an able and faithful minister. Be sure you take care the person be orthodox in the faith, and of blameless life, and does own the confession put forth by our brethren in London in 1689.[3]

At one time, Screven's sermons must have been available for study. Oliver Hart, who became pastor of the Charleston church in 1750, wrote of Screven:

> His talents were above mediocrity, though favored with but a partial literary competency, yet a brilliant and energetic imagination, a fervent heart, enlivened by the genial influence of Christianity wonderfully aided him. He was beloved by his brethren, his ministrations were listened to with delight and received with edification and profit. He was eminent for devoted piety and religious usefulness.[4]

---

3. James P. Wesberry, *The Life and Work of William Screven, Father of Southern Baptists* (Privately printed, 1941).

4. Oliver Hart, *Diary of Rev. Oliver Hart,* Vol. I.

In this brief paragraph, Hart may well have assessed a majority of Baptist preaching and preachers in the South for his day,
for our day, and for all the days in between.

FRANCIS PELOT (1720-?)

Francis Pelot was fourteen-years-old, extremely well educated
for his day, and a native of Switzerland when he arrived in South
Carolina in 1734. He was ordained by the Euhaw Baptist Church
in South Carolina January 13, 1752. After his ordination, Pelot
became pastor of the Euhaw church and continued in that position until his death.

Pelot wrote the oldest Baptist sermon manuscript available
on February 26, 1759, for the ordination of Samuel Stillman and
Nicholas Bedgegood. The entire service took place, according to
a note on the last page, "at the Baptist men's meeting house in
Charleston." The original manuscript is in the Furman University Library. He titled the sermon, with text from Isaiah 6:8 and
Acts 13:2, "The Qualified Christian Separated to the Work of the
Ministry." Clear and eminently practical, the sermon included
two major divisions, with each division having an obvious textual basis: (1) Qualified Christians are such as are properly separated, (Isa. 6:8) and (2) Qualified Christians are such as faithfully
perform the duties of the sacred function to which they are
called (Acts 13:2).

Pelot's sermon began with a reference to soteriology, which,
as we have already noted, was a key doctrinal issue for his day.

> As soon as Adam had fallen . . . in which he stood as the Repre-
> sentative of mankind; God in love and mercy was pleased to reveal
> unto him the covenant of grace, which was established in Christ
> from eternity, whereby his sinking and distressed soul was made to
> hope for peace and reconciliation.

The Regular Baptist influence in Pelot is obvious in the logical progression and the theological depth of the sermon. Both
are evident in the outline of the sermon. Notice that the key
word in point one is "separated." This word is repeated consecutively in the subpoints. This repetitive process assists the con-

gregation in following and in retaining the development and the emphases of the sermon.

I. They are Such as are Properly Separated:

1. A faithful and well qualified Gospel minister is separated from siners [sic] as Christ our great example was. We do not mean absence by separation; no, ministers are even to seek after them as poor lost sheep. Luke 15:2. But by a separation from sinners we understand a separation "from sinners evil ways."

2. A faithful Gospel minister is separated from the vanity of the times. And if ever they need to be skillful, it is when they hurl a blow at those darling vanities, especially as some professors (of the faith) give sanction to them.

3. A faithful Gospel minister is separated by grace; otherwise, he would be no more than the blind leading the blind.

4. A minister properly separated, ought to have some distinguished gifts both natural and acquired for except he be furnished with these talents how shall he speak either in private or public?

5. A minister ought to be separated by his church. He must prove himself before them.[5]

Point II had the same logical development as point I, but seemed to have lost some of the careful precision of point I. Repetition is obvious in point II, but it is not as strong as it was in point I.

II. They are such as faithfully perform the duties of the sacred function to which they are called.

1. They are said to be salt, (Matt. 5:13).

2. They are said to be light, (Matt. 5:14-16).

3. They are said to be shepherds, (Jer. 23:4) "I shall set up shepherds over them which shall feed them. Therefore it is the undoubted duty of ministers to feed the Lord's children with the wholesome word of truth, and to exercise the most tender cares over them that are the objects of Christ's grace and love.

4. A gospel minister is also said to be a steward, (1 Cor. 2:1).

5. They are said to be watchmen, (Ezek. 3:17).

6. Ministers are said to be calmers, (1 Cor. 3:9).

---

5. Cecil Edwin Sherman, "A History of Baptist Preaching in the South Before 1845" (Ft. Worth: Th.D. dissertation, Southwestern Baptist Theological Seminary, 1960), 36.

Pelot's sermon was brief by the standards of the eighteenth century. However, the sermon was only one part of the ordination service, and Pelot may have felt that a forty-five to sixty minute sermon was adequate for the occasion.

Some other specific evidence exists that Pelot studied diligently. The Furman University Library also owns a copy of John Gill's *A Collection of the Sermons and Tracts*. The flyleaf indicates that the original owner of the book was Francis Pelot. The book is marked frequently where Pelot sought to increase his understanding of preaching.

Of Francis Pelot, Oliver Hart wrote:

> As to his preaching he did not content himself with delivering a little dry morality, but unfolded and applyed the great and glorious doctrine of the Gospel. His principles were truly evangelical. . . .[6]

Oliver Hart (1723-1795)

Oliver Hart conscientiously recorded many details of his life. We know from Hart's own pen that he ". . . was born July ye 5th 1723 in Westminister Township, Bucks County and province of Pennsylvania." Not surprisingly, then, we find in Hart's diary that he ". . . was called to and accepted of the pastoral charge of the Baptist church of Charles Town Feb. ye 16th 1750." Hart served the church until 1780 when he fled arrest by British troops. He pastored a Baptist church in Hopewell, New Jersey, from 1780 until his death on December 31, 1795.

Hart's Bible, his diary, and many other of his papers, including sermons and sermon outlines are located in the South Caroliniana Library in Columbia, near the University of South Carolina. His sermons seem highly pedestrian in that there is little sense of imagination evident, nor is there much about his sermons that would provoke thought. Hart's strength lay in his ability to speak plain, simple language.

The outline of a sermon preached October 20, 1757, is typical of Hart's preaching. The orderliness of the sermon indicates that Hart was a Regular Baptist, but without the flair of Pelot:

6. Hart, *Diary*.

2 Tim. 1:9

1st shew wt is meant by this Call wth wch . . . ye Apostle has called
us

2nd shew what kind of Call it is

Lastly improve ye whole

1st What is meant by this Call and c.

There is an external call

an internal

2 Gen. what kind of a Call this is

1st an all powerful efficacious Call

2 an Holy Calling

3 Not according to our works

4 But according to His purpose

5 According to His Grace

6 This Grace was given to us before the world began

Titus 1:2

Apply

1 What hath been said reproves such who denies ye powerfull
unfrustratable operations of ye Spirit in Salvation.

2 Have you experienced this Inward Call if not on to those who
have.[7]

Hart's sermons were primarily topical in the best sense of that
word. He stayed with the biblical idea, but was extremely limited
in the exposition of the text.

Richard Furman eulogized Hart in 1796 with a mixture of
praise and frankness.

> His sermons were peculiarly serious, containing a happy assem-
> blage of doctrinal and practical truths, set in an engaging light, and
> enforced with convincing arguments. . . . His eloquence . . . was not
> of the most popular kind.[8]

---

7. Ibid.
8. Quoted by William B. Sprague, *Annals of the American Pulpit*, VI (New York: Robert Carter & Bros., 1860), 49.

David Thomas (1732-1801)

David Thomas was of Regular Baptist persuasion. He was educated, dignified, poised, polished, widely respected by famous men such as Benjamin Franklin and also by the uneducated, rural, noncosmopolitan people of the colony of Virginia. Thomas was born in Pennsylvania in 1732 and educated at Isaac Eaton's School in Hopewell, New Jersey. Probably as a result of appeals that he had heard at a meeting of the Philadelphia Baptist Association, Thomas visited Fauquier County, Virginia. He found a mission field filled with people who had yet to hear an evangelical message.

Thomas perceived that God would use him as a pioneer evangelist and church founder. Whether by purpose or by accident, Thomas virtually imitated the apostle Paul's missionary journeys to key settlements throughout Virginia. Churches were founded in Fauquier County, Champawansick, Loudon County on the Little River, Orange County, and at Accaquan. Thomas preached in many other churches and places and corresponded with them.

Thomas also made an important contribution to Baptist thought as an author. When persecution of Baptists intensified, Thomas wrote *The Virginian Baptist*. This defense of the Baptists was the first published account of Baptist doctrine to appear in the South. The book is a classic. Thomas deals with Baptist doctrines, Baptist polity, and various objections made against Baptists. The value of Thomas' education is evident in his statement on the church:

> The Greek substantive so often used in the *New Testament,* and always translated the Church, or an assembly, is evidently derived of a verb that signifies "to be called out." It must therefore certainly refer to something that is possessed of life, and is capable of hearing, understanding, and obeying a vocation or command. So that the Gospel-Church, must signify a company of persons removed in compliance with some call. "Tis customary indeed in some places, to call the house dedicated to divine service, 'the Church:'" But this is not according to Scripture. The inspired writers as far as I can remember never use the word in that sense. Wherefore, it properly refers to the people, and not the building where they meet to wor-

ship. Hence we are told in the Prayerbook, that "the Church of CHRIST is an assembly of faithful men." Which though short, is I think when fully understood, a very just description of it.[9]

David Thomas may well have been an outstanding Baptist preacher in America in the eighteenth century. Unfortunately, none of his sermons are available to us today.

Shubal Stearns (1706-1771)

Shubal Stearns, a Separate Baptist, was a product of the Great Awakening of the eighteenth century. He was born in Boston in 1706, and was "born again" in 1745 during a sermon by George Whitefield. He joined the Baptist church at Tolland, Connecticut in 1751. Years before David Thomas served rural communities in Virginia, Shubal Stearns was busy preaching in the backwoods of Virginia, North Carolina, South Carolina, and finally in Georgia. His zeal and plain speaking became a model for Baptist preachers in the South for decades.

Stearns lacked formal education, but studied privately. Unpublished historical materials, gathered by Morgan Edwards, give us strong glimpses into the heart and preaching of Stearns. Edwards frankly asserts: "Of learning he (Stearns) had but a small share, yet was pretty well acquainted with books." Edwards graphically described Stearn's delivery and the strong influence Stearns had on other preachers.

> His voice was musical and strong, which he managed in such a manner as, one while, to make soft impressions on the heart, and fetch tears from the eyes in a mechanical way; and anon, to shake the very nerves and throw the animal system into tumults and purturbations. All the Separate ministers copy after him in tones of voice and actions of body; and some few exceed him.[10]

Stearns probably sounded much like George Whitefield.

---

9. David Thomas, *The Virginian Baptist* (Baltimore: Enoch Story, 1774), 23. Cecil Sherman used this excerpt in his dissertation. After reading David Thomas, I agree with Sherman that this excerpt is not only representative, but also excellently written.

10. Morgan Edwards, "Materials Towards the History of Baptists in the Province of Virginia," Vol. IV, unpublished, 21.

Stearns likely never prepared sermon manuscripts, and perhaps never preached using notes. Separate Baptist preachers were given much to the immediate moving of the Spirit during the sermon, and given to preaching with unction and zeal rather than with study and preparation. No sermon manuscripts, notes, or even quotes from Stearns' sermons are available to us.

Philip Mulkey (1732-1805)

Philip Mulkey was a deeply, and possibly darkly, Christian mystic. An oral tradition, the accuracy of which was attested by several people, that relates a little of Mulkey's conversion experience, is representative of Mulkey's mysticism.

> One night as he went out of a house where he had been playing the fiddle at a dancing frolic, he saw (as he thought) the Devil grinning at him with fiery eyes, upon which he swooned away. When he came to himself, he was in the greatest terror, thinking the Devil would be permitted to take him away bodily by way of example to the company he had been with. However, he mounted his horse and as he rode home, fancied that the trees struck at him, and the stars frowned at him. In this terror he continued about three weeks, reforming, but not able to sleep much, and wasting in flesh and strength.[11]

Mulkey was baptized by Shubal Stearns on Christmas, 1756. Less than a year later, he was ordained and began pastoring the Deep River Baptist Church in North Carolina. Mulkey and thirteen members of that church moved to South Carolina and eventually settled at Fairforest where a meetinghouse was built.

Mulkey's ministry was one of missionary intensity. Five churches were started by Fairforest, and many other churches were given personal and financial assistance. Like David Thomas and Shubal Stearns, Mulkey found many people who had never heard an evangelical witness. All three of these ministers served in fields that were "white unto harvest."

None of Mulkey's sermons are available to us.

---

11. James Davis Bailey, *"Reverends Philip Mulkey and James Fowler: The Story of the First Baptist Church Planted in Upper South Carolina,"* n.p, 3.

Daniel Marshall (1706-1784)

Daniel Marshall, like Stearns, Thomas, and others of the early
preachers in the South, was a New Englander. He was born in a
Christian home in Windsor, Connecticut, in 1706. Converted in
1726, he was inspired, during one of George Whitefield's sermons, to become a missionary to the Mohawk Indians. Eighteen
months later (with or without the good wishes of the Mohawks)
he changed his mind and decided to join the Stearns group in
Virginia and become a Baptist. Marshall continued to have trou-
ble locating a suitable place of service until 1770. At that time,
he was arrested for preaching in Georgia. This religious intoler-
ance somehow inspired Marshall. Even though the court ordered him to ". . . come into Georgia no more, as a preacher," a
few weeks later, on January 1, 1771, Marshall began preaching
at a settlement near Augusta. By the spring of 1771, the Kiokee
Baptist Church was formed. That church is not only in existence
today but it is thriving at a site not too far from its original location.

Marshall was a determined man, and an indefatigable worker
who openly witnessed wherever he could find people. He appeared in market places, at races, army camps, and homes pro-
claiming the gospel. Like Stearns, Marshall probably never
wrote a sermon manuscript or sermon notes, and was given to
the immediacy of the Spirit. No portions of any of Marshall's sermons are available to us today.

John Leland (1754-1841)

John Leland was born in Grafton, Massachusetts, May 14,
1754. He was baptized in 1774, and soon after began one of the
most vigorous preaching careers Baptists have ever witnessed.
Itinerant preachers such as Leland were known as "volunteers
for Christ." He testified that in his younger days he preached
twelve to fourteen times a week, especially in Orange, Louisa,
Culpepper, and Spotsylvania Counties of Virginia where he had
moved in 1776. Leland combined Regular and Separate Baptist
tendencies. His Regular Baptist leanings are evident because he

was an organized and disciplined person not averse to study and learning. His sermons were clear and thoroughly organized. Leland, however, liked the Separatist tendencies toward informality.

Leland's wide travels gave him a lot of influence in Virginia, and that added to his credibility with men such as Thomas Jefferson and James Madison. Leland's famous campaign for what eventually became the Bill of Rights has been widely recorded. Jefferson found that through Leland, he could feel the pulse of the people. Somewhat sardonically, Jefferson admitted that through Leland, the people could feel the pulse of Jefferson. Leland's credibility with the people and with the aspiring leaders of the new nation brought a dramatic increase of respect to Baptists.

He was a practical and plain-spoken preacher. His sermons were extremely thought provoking, intellectually challenging, built on logical analysis and are a delight to read. The titles of Leland's sermons were attention getting. Examples include, "The Jarring Interests of Heaven" (Col. 1:20, the sermon was built on a suggestion from the text) and "Blow at the Root" (no text announced, but several references to Scripture within the sermon). Leland kept his congregations spellbound.

Leland's use of the Bible in his preaching ranged from occasional direct exposition of the text, to building a topical sermon from a general suggestion in the text, to announcing no specific text.

One of Leland's favorite subjects was religious liberty. The sermon "Blow at the Root" was designed to destroy the concept that government should ever devise laws to manage religious practice. Leland specifically addressed a Massachusetts law that ordered all Massachusetts towns to have a "meeting house" (church building) and a "teacher" (pastor). Fines were to be levied against towns not complying with this law.

Leland's sermon "Blow at the Root" defies any attempt to summarize, capsule, or reduce it to an expanded outline. The thought processes are intricately woven together. In this sermon, Leland used homely illustrations, various forms of argumentation (which appealed to the desire for intellectual exercise among the congregants), vivid descriptions, and plain language. The use of plain, simple language was obvious throughout the sermon. The use of homely illustrations occurred in the opening paragraphs of the sermon:

> Man comes into the world *needy, dependant* (sic), *frail,* and *polluted.* He is born without clothes and shoes, and with his mouth opened by a craving appetite. These needs have given rise to the various arts so studiously and gradualy learnt among men.
>
> The need of a shirt has set the farmer to work to raise his flax, and the woman to spin and weave it; which again has set others to work to make tools for the farmer, spinner, and weaver to perform with.

Leland continued this theme of interdependence showing that all freedom necessarily entailed responsibilities and limitations. The responsibilities and limitations needed to be understood by citizens, and especially by legislators. The specific concerns of the sermon were addressed.

> Reflect a moment, how cruel it is to fine a town or parish for not having a teacher, when none but God can make them teachers; and that those who are sent of God to preach, feel a necessity to preach, not only without the support of law, but in opposition thereto; obeying God rather than man.
>
> It is so strange a thing, that in Massachusetts, where the people are so versant in the New Testament, they should make and submit to such laws, that if I did not know it to be a fact, I would not believe a report of it.
> There are three reasons offered, why religion should be established by the laws of men, viz.
>
> First, to prevent error.
>
> Second, to effect and preserve uniformity of sentiment.
>
> Third, To support the Gospel.
>
> . . .To support the Gospel. That is, to raise money by law, equalized upon all people, for the purpose of building meeting-houses, paying preachers, and etc. Building temples for religious worship seems to be a prudential thing. . . .but the question is, whether this

money is to be collected by *legal force or moral obligation?* If by *legal force,* then the principle is supported, that the cause of God is to be directed and supported by the laws of man; and of course all the persecutions mentioned before, are justifiable. . . .Pray tell me where Jesus or the apostles ever called upon the rulers of state to make any laws to oblige people to part with their money to hire preachers or build meeting houses? I am serious: I am in earnest: if our present edition (of the Bible) is not complete, search the original, and put your finger on the passage. I have not yet seen it, and until I do, I shall call all such laws anti-scriptural and anti-Christian.

The following excerpt from the same sermon used argumentation by reducing the specious law to the absurd:

How often I have wished, that when rulers undertake to make laws about religion, they would complete the code; not only make provision for building meeting-houses, paying preachers, and forcing people to hear them; but also to enjoin on the hearers repentance, faith, self-denial, love to God, and love to man. That everyone who did not repent of his sins should pay five pounds. That all those who did not believe, should pay ten pounds. That every soul who did not deny himself and take up his cross daily, should pay fifteen pounds. That whoever did not love God with all his heart should be imprisoned a year. And that if a man did not love his neighbor as himself, he should be confined for life.

That all these duties are taught in the New Testament is certain; if, therefore, the laws of man are to enjoin moral duties, this important one should not be neglected: but on only hearing of them, our minds are struck with the absurdity of reducing them to civil legislation and jurisprudence; and had not the poison of anti-Christ infected the minds of men, they would be equally struck with the making of human laws about any religious article.[12]

These excerpts are a mere sampling of the genius of Leland. His sermons make pertinent reading and preaching today just as they did in his day.

---

12. John Leland, *Blow at the Root* (New London: Joseph D. Huntington, 1801), 10.

SAMUEl HARRiss (1724-1799)

Samuel Harriss was born in 1724 in Virginia to a wealthy Baptist family. He became a Separate Baptist in 1758, and almost immediately began an evangelistic preaching tour of southern Virginia and northern North Carolina. His preaching evidently impressed some people, because in 1774 he was elected an "apostle" by the General Association of Baptists in Virginia. (In 1774 the General Association determined that this New Testament title should continue to be used in modern churches. The title was officially dropped a few months later.) Harriss endured in the work so faithfully that he was instrumental in the founding of twenty-six Baptist churches in Virginia.

The only record we have of his preaching is found in a quote by Robert Semple:

> As a doctrinal preacher, his talents were rather below mediocrity; unless at those times when he was highly favored from above, then he would sometimes display considerable ingenuity. His excellency consisted chiefly in addressing the heart; and perhaps even Whitefield did not surpass him in this respect. When animated himself, he seldom failed to animate his auditory.[13]

Lewis LuNsfoRd (1753-1793)

Lewis Lunsford, a Regular Baptist, combined homiletic eloquence with medical skills in his work for the Lord in northern Virginia. He was born in Stafford County in 1753. There is a record of him preaching to large crowds by 1770. Although we know of no early formal education for Lunsford, he was a supporter of educational institutions. The Moratico Baptist Church, where Lunsford was pastor, sent money to Rhode Island College at a time when most Virginia Baptists saw little need for an "educated pulpit." Lunsford, as Leland, was opposed to slavery; despite this and his support for educational institutions, Lunsford was held in high esteem.

---

13. Quoted by James B. Taylor, *Virginia Baptist Ministers,* I (New York: Sheldon & Co., 1860), 34.

None of Lunsford's sermons are available to us, but there were many complimentary testimonies about his preaching. This excerpt from one of his eulogies is representative.

> With what pungency did he preach the word; what energy clothed his expression; what powers of argument flowed thro' his lips; what earnestness streamed from his eyes; and what music dwelt upon his tongue while to surrounding, gazing, weeping and rejoicing multitudes he preached as if he ne'er would preach again.[14]

LEMUEL BURKITT (1750-1807)

Lemuel Burkitt's preaching helped bring desperately needed doctrinal stability to North Carolina. The influence of General Baptists in North Carolina had a tragic legacy. Several churches had baptized people who were admittedly nonbelievers. Others were baptized before their conversion experience. Burkitt took a strong General Baptist stance and preached powerfully in advocating the baptism of believers only.

Burkitt was born in North Carolina in 1750. From 1770 to 1804, he was pastor of Sandy Run Baptist Church. In 1801, he traveled to Kentucky to witness the outbreak of a great revival. He was revived, and brought a new evangelistic commitment to his preaching; North Carolina also experienced a great revival.

There are no sermons by Burkitt available to us. The best description of his preaching is included in the minutes of the North Carolina Chowan Association.

> He was a man of strong mind, well acquainted with men and things, a close reasoner, and was remarkably methodical in the arrangement of his discourses; his manner was bold, yet very persuasive and pathetic. His voice was rather weak and effiminate [sic], and it was often difficult, and sometimes, in large congregations, impossible to make himself heard by all; yet there was frequently under his preaching, a very visible display of Divine power among the people, toward the close of his discourses, when the tears would copiously roll from his eyes, and all *that* flowing from his tongue,

14. Quoted by Garnett Ryland, *The Baptists of Virginia 1699-1926*, (Richmond, Va.: Baptist Board of Missions and Education, 1955), 118.

which was calculated to move, melt and engage the heart of man, it was next to impossible to remain unaffected. . . .[15]

Edmund Botsford (1745-1819)

Edmund Botsford was England-born, but America-adopted. He came to Charleston, South Carolina, around 1770. Despite early Baptist guidance by an aunt, when Botsford arrived in Charleston he was known as a public "idler and wastrel." Fortunately, Botsford met Oliver Hart and his early training was rekindled. After Botsford became a Christian, he was called to preach. He studied under Hart and was ordained as a minister in 1772. His love for America grew and he became a chaplain to American soldiers in South Carolina and Georgia.

At first, Botsford was an itinerant preacher. He traveled so much that he became known as "the flying preacher." By 1797, he settled down as pastor in Georgetown, South Carolina, and served the church there until he died in 1819.

Botsford's sermons are not available to us. A rare testimony by Botsford on sermon delivery style, however, is available.

> Mr. Botsford frequently used notes in preaching — sometimes pretty copious ones. But he was never a *reader* of sermons. Referring to some of his young brethren who were in the habit of reading their discourses, he thus writes to a friend: — "It surely never was the design of our Master that his servants should *read* the Gospel when he said, 'Go, preach.' Do you say Dr. Stillman writes all his sermons? But Dr. Stillman does not read his sermons. I mean not to object against writing, but reading. I hope you will use your influence to persuade young gentlemen to lay aside their crutches by degrees.[16]

Abraham Marshall (1745-1819)

With some pride, Abraham Marshall liked to share that he had received a total of only forty days of schooling. To his credit, Marshall made no comparison, as some have, between his forty days of schooling and the forty days Jesus was tempted. Marshall

15. *Minutes of the North Carolina Chowan Baptist Association* (Elizabeth City: Joseph Beasley, 1808), 4.
16. Sprague, 144.

was the son of Daniel Marshall and the maternal nephew of Shubal Stearns. Both heredity and environment conjoined to make Abraham Marshall a Separate Baptist.

In 1789, Marshall had won the trust of Georgians and was named a member of the Georgia Constitutional Convention. Surprisingly, he later became a trustee of Franklin College (which later became the University of Georgia). Obviously, Marshall developed an appreciation for formal education despite his much publicized lack of it.

One sermon by Abraham Marshall is available to us. He preached that sermon at Franklin College in 1815. The text was a launch pad from which several somewhat disparate ideas were explored. The sermon was taken from 2 Kings 6:6 with the title "The Iron Did Swim." The introduction of the sermon affirms Marshall's belief in supernatural miracles. The sermon is rather plain in its development with three points.

     I A few remarks on miracles in general.
   II. Consider the miracle embraced in the text with a few neighboring ones.
  III. A few inferences on the whole.

Point III is developed in a curious way:

1. God is in favor of education: this can be deduced because this miracle was performed before a *school* of prophets.
2. Our holy religion was abetted by men of education.
3. Our nation needs young men of wisdom.
4. Seek wisdom that comes from a knowledge of Jesus Christ.

Marshall's forty days of schooling were obviously complemented by his own native intellectual abilities.

Richard Furman (1755-1825)

In many ways, good and bad, Richard Furman was born *for* his time. More than anyone else in Baptist history, Furman brought unity and vision to Baptists during a time Baptists lacked both. He brought unity by drawing Regular Baptists and Separate Baptists together in theology and polity. As a man for his time, Furman brought vision to Baptists on the need for an educated clergy. Those were his good contributions. Unfortunately, as a man *of* his time, Furman adamantly supported the institution of slavery.

How did it happen that Richard Furman became a man who would shape, guide and influence Baptists, Baptist education, and Baptist preaching to this day?

Furman was born into a Regular Baptist family on October 9, 1755, in Esopus, New York. Evidently, the Furman family had long planned a move to Charleston, South Carolina, and as soon as Richard and his mother were strong enough to travel, the move was made. The Furmans attended the Charleston Baptist Church and became close friends of the pastor, Oliver Hart. They later moved to High Hills of Santee (now known as Santee) and joined a Separate Baptist Church. Probably due to the strong encouragement of the Furmans, Hart, a Regular Baptist, preached at Santee on several occasions. As a teen-ager, Richard Furman was exposed not only to two Baptist ways of thinking, he also witnessed how those two camps were finding collegiality and common ground.

In 1771, Joseph Reese, a Separate Baptist who had been converted during a sermon by Shubal Stearns, preached at High Hills. The Separate Baptists placed immense importance, as we have noted, on soteriology. When he was fifteen years old, Richard Furman was converted during Reese's preaching. He brought his Regular Baptist upbringing under Oliver Hart and added to that his conversion experience under Separate Baptist Reese. Furman continued to endear himself to both groups as he became a hardworking, evangelistic preacher. In addition to his evangelistic work, Furman served as pastor of High Hills from 1774-1787. In 1787, he was called as pastor of the Charleston church where he served until his death in 1825.

Furman used his Regular Baptist inclination for organizing and his Separate Baptist zeal for campaigning to bring about denominational unity. He led in the advancement of the Triennial Convention, which greatly improved Baptist cooperative efforts in missions, not only in South Carolina, but throughout the colonies. Furman also organized the first state-wide meeting of Baptists in the South in South Carolina. William Bullein

Johnson, who later became the first president of the Southern Baptist Convention, carefully observed Furman at work. Almost despite themselves, Regular and Separate Baptists found that they could maintain some diversity while cooperating on missions. This foundation of unity amid diversity would be characteristic of Baptists in the South for nearly two centuries.

Furman's parents cultivated in him an appreciation for an educated ministry. He learned to read from the Bible. His father instructed him in mathematics, sciences, and business. Obviously a gifted child, he also studied Latin, Greek, and Hebrew on his own. Oliver Hart probably instructed him in theology, at least until 1780. Furman was so adamant in his insistence on education for ministers that South Carolinians really had little choice but to name a college (Furman University, Greenville) after him. In fact, Furman was indirectly responsible for the founding of Mercer University. It was Furman who persuaded Silas Mercer to change his views from anti-education to pro-education. As a result, Silas Mercer's son, Jesse, was deeply affected by Furman's commitment to education. Mercer University in Macon, Georgia, is the direct result of that influence.

A few of Furman's sermons have been preserved. The sermons had an announced text and the relationship between the text and the sermon was always strong and clear. His sermons were well-organized and scholarly in that they reflected an awareness of historical background of the text, and of linguistic matters in the text. The last "point" of his sermons was applications to his congregation.

Furman used lofty language, deep and intricate development of his views, and extensive apologetics in defense of his patriotism, and in defense of his pro-slavery views.

The sermon "America's Deliverance and Duty"[17] was of special interest since it was preached July 4, 1802. Furman was at his best in this sermon, combining biblical exposition with specific applications to his day, especially as they related to patriotism.

17. Richard Furman, *America's Deliverance and Duty* (Charleston: W.P. Young, 1802), 5-22.

Text: Exodus 13:3

Introduction: The children of Israel groaned under oppression. Eventually, by the outstretched hand of Omnipotence, their deliverance was effected.

To impress them with a due sense of their obligations to infinite goodness; and to commemorate their deliverance, this ransomed people were commanded to consecrate the day as a sacred festival, to be kept by them and succeeding generations.

On this anniversary of our independence, therefore, permit to attempt showing:

I. That there is great reason to believe, the American Revolution was effected by the special agency of God. The justice of our cause, both in a moral and a political sense, forms a strong argument in our favor. Also, the contest was entered with much scrupulosity and reluctance. Our army, untrained, needed special grace to overcome the powerful British army. The war was terminated in a way truly glorious to America. From what has transpired it seems reasonable to conclude that God designed America as an asylum for religious liberty.

II. The duties incumbent on our citizens in consequence of God's gracious interposition: Give honor to God; give strict attention to religion; live virtuously; share the gospel; be a conscientious citizen.

An early biography of Furman cited his preaching as:

Combining efforts of intellect, memory, judgment, personal advantages of figure, countenance and voice, he was in preaching peculiarly impressive; at once exemplifying the benevolent spirit of the gospel and inculcating its precepts with energy that commanded the respect of all.[18]

Furman made a stalwart defense of slavery. Loulie Latimer Owens Pettigrew, in her insightful book, *Saints of Clay,* notes that in the early 1800's Furman termed slavery "undoubtedly an evil." In December of 1822, however, Furman wrote a lengthy treatise on the biblical justification of slavery. His arguments in favor of slavery became the base from which many discourses, including numerous sermons, would attempt to justify slavery.

18. Harvey T. Cook, *A Biography of Richard Furman* (Greenville: Baptist Courier Jot Rooms, 1913), 8-9.

Representative of these discourses is a sermon preached in Charleston in 1850 which will be cited in the next chapter.

Jonathan Maxcy (1768-1820)

Among the highest tributes given to a preacher in the nineteenth century were those given to Jonathan Maxcy, a Regular Baptist. Maxcy was born in Massachusetts on September 2, 1768. His family was able to afford the finest education for him. After attending Wrentham Academy and graduating from Rhode Island College, Jonathan Maxcy became, in succession, tutor, librarian, professor of divinity, president pro-tem, and president of Rhode Island College. Simultaneous to his service as college president, Maxcy also served as pastor of the prestigious First Baptist Church of Providence.

He served as president of Union College in Schenectady, New York from 1802 to 1804. At the urging of Richard Furman, Maxcy accepted the presidency of South Carolina College, where he served from 1804 until his death in 1820. To this day, Maxcy College is a part of the University of South Carolina.

The tributes to Maxcy as a preacher are outstanding. In his eulogy, Robert Henry declared: "Dr. Maxcy's great fame, as a professor, was, doubtless, much assisted by his uncommon celebrity as a preacher." Congressman James Pettigru said, "Never will the charm of his eloquence be erased from my memory." A South Carolina judge averred, "His . . . sermons were the finest specimens of eloquence and truth to which I have ever listened." Senator Evans felt that Maxcy ". . . was . . . the greatest orator I have ever heard." And in his memoirs, a preacher named William T. Brantly wrote: "His preaching possessed a power and charm which we have never witnessed, to the same extent, in any other man."

The sermon, "The Existence of God Demonstrated from the Works of Creation," exemplified all of these noble attributes. This sermon reflected a high view of Scripture and developed the text in a direct and forthright manner. A summary of that sermon will give us a glimpse of Maxcy's preaching style:

Text: Romans 1:20

Introduction:

Nothing will more effectually guard us against vice, than a firm belief in the existence of God.

Our happiness depends on our virtue. Our virtue depends on the conformity of our hearts and conduct to the laws prescribed us by our beneficent Creator.

A belief in the existence of God is the true original source of all virtue, and the only foundation of all religion, natural or revealed. Set aside this great luminous truth, erase the conviction of it from the heart, you then place virtue and vice on the same level.

I. Man himself is a proof of God's existence.

Man surely could not, as has been vainly and idly supposed, have been formed by the fortuitous concurrence of atoms.

That intelligence which directed the orderly formation of the human body must have resided in a Being whose power was adequate to the production of such an effect.

II. The earth is proof of God's existence.

III. The oceans are proof of God's existence.

IV. The air that surrounds the earth is proof of God's existence.

V. The firmament of heaven declares God's handy work.

Conclusion:

This great Being is everywhere present. He exists all around us.

The most prominent features of this are exhibited in that incomprehensible display of wisdom, power and goodness, made in the works of creation.[19]

Obviously, Maxcy deserved the high tribute he received as a preacher.

William T. Brantly, Sr. (1787-1845)

William T. Brantly was born in Chatham County, North Carolina, January 23, 1787. He was converted in 1802. Immediately after his baptism, Brantly sought permission to preach to the congregation. The new young preacher evidently impressed the congregation with his passion for preaching.

---

19. Romeo Elton, ed. *The Literary Remains of the Rev. Jonathan Maxcy* (New York: A.V. Blake, 1844), 43-50.

Brantly quietly personified Regular Baptist and perhaps all Baptist preaching in the South at its best. The themes of Brantly's sermons were always a step above the obvious or mundane. His outlines were clear and had appeal for people at every socio-educational level. He was generous in spirit to those who disagreed with him theologically. Such an attitude was uncharacteristic of Baptist preaching in the South in the nineteenth century.

Brantly had the good fortune to study under Jonathan Maxcy at South Carolina College. The influence of Maxcy was reflected in the depth of thought given by Brantly to his sermons. In 1809, while serving as rector of Richmond Academy in Augusta, Georgia, Brantly helped found the First Baptist Church. He served as pastor of the Beaufort Baptist Church from 1811 to 1818. He returned to Augusta on May 6, 1821, and preached the dedication service for the first church building of the First Baptist Church of that city. Brantly served as pastor of First Baptist Church, Philadelphia, from 1826 to 1837, and First Baptist Church, Charleston, South Carolina, from 1837 to 1845.

The sermon Brantly preached for the dedication of the new building at Augusta is a perfect model of the skills he used in preaching. This sermon, by the most prevalent definitions of our day, cannot be called an expository sermon. It wove the poetic inspiration and beauty of the text and applied that inspiration and beauty to a contemporary congregation. Whether the sermon was expository or not, it reflected a superior use of Scripture in preaching.

> Title: "The Beauty and Stability of Gospel Institutions"
> Text:Psalm 90:17
> Introduction:
> Since man is a dying creature, all that man builds takes on his mortality. Thus, our new building will decay as do we. But the light of eternity imparts a genuine glory to the events of our being; and the works of our hands . . . acquire perpetuity.
> I. On the truth and certainty of the doctrine of which this church is the repository: the doctrines announced in this church have a wonderful correspondence with our actual condition.

II. On the approving tokens of divine regard: the success of the work of the Kingdom of God indicates God's favor on the general plan.

III. On the imparted beauty of our Lord: the beauty of the Lord through His great salvation will give stability to this church.[20]

Brantly closed with comments that still shout to be heard.

> Friends and brethren of other denominations, who have assisted us in the erection of this house, we have now set before you a hasty sketch of the principles by which we intend to regulate our ministry in this place. We court no invidious distinctions—we seek no pre-eminence. Wishing to be identified with those who are fellow-workers together with God, we receive with Christian satisfaction the friendly countenance with which you have beheld this work. Let us cultivate the spirit of brotherly love, and live as one community. Our circumstantial differences should not influence the opinion which we form of each other. These minor shades will soon be lost in the blaze of ultimate glory. As expectants of one heaven, and followers of one Lord, let us unite for the common interests of Zion. We have enemies enough from without, and should therefore cultivate the spirit of benevolence among ourselves.[21]

Amen! and Amen, again!

JESSE MERCER (1769-1841)

Jesse Mercer was given every educational opportunity available to a young man in eighteenth-century Georgia. He decided that those opportunities were too limited in scope and availability and he did something about it. Throughout his adult life, Mercer worked to establish a college in Georgia. Not surprisingly, the college is now known as Mercer University.

Mercer was born in Halifax County, North Carolina, December 16, 1769. In 1785, he was baptized at the Kiokee church near Augusta. In 1788, he was ordained to preach and at one time pastored four Baptist churches simultaneously.

In addition to his educational and pastoral work, Mercer led in the development of the Georgia Baptist Convention. He also

20. William T. Brantly, "The Beauty and Stability of Gospel Institutions," *Georgia Baptist Pulpit, I*, 215-223.
21. Ibid., 223.

supported missions, the Triennial Convention, and *The Christian Index,* which he purchased with his own money and then donated it to the Georgia Baptist Convention.

Mercer's sermons were highly analytical. If the sermon outlines available to us are accurate (and they probably are), his sermons were logical, but tedious in their detail. He used very little illustrative material except for quotations to advance his arguments and to relieve the steady flow of information. Mercer's sermons occasionally demonstrated a high view of Scripture, but he was not above the practice of occasionally bending his text to fit his sermon idea. Most of his sermons were designed to inform or change an attitude. Few, if any, of Mercer's sermons were designed to inspire. Mercer used typology on occasion. He was solidly against open communion.

Mercer's campaign for ministerial education, of course, found its way into his preaching. For example, consider this sermon which is indicative of Mercer in what are his best uses of the biblical text in a sermon:

> Text: 2 Corinthians 6:1-10
>
> Title: Knowledge Indispensable to a Minister of God
>
> Introduction: The minister's very calling requires him to give his best. Purity and knowledge are the two most important to justify claims of being a true minister.
>
> I. What kind of knowledge is necessary to a minister? The knowledge of truth. In Jesus abides all truth.
>
> II. How is such knowledge attained? Not easily. Only patient and persevering efforts will gain such knowledge. Even Solomon had to search for wisdom. Other biblical men worked hard in study to qualify for service.
>
> III. The writers of the Bible books were men of sound learning.[22]

Other Preachers

Many other preachers made contributions to Baptist life before the Southern Baptist Convention was organized.

---

22. Jesse Mercer, "Knowledge Indispensable to a Minister of God," *Georgia Baptist Pulpit,* ed. Robert Fleming, I (Richmond: H.K. Ellyson, 1847), 9-19.

Andrew Broaddus

Andrew Broaddus was a teaching type preacher who was more at ease in rural settings than in cities. Broaddus pastored the First Baptist Church of Richmond, Virginia, for a brief time. He resigned to return to church service in nonmetropolitan areas. Most Baptist preachers in the eighteenth and early nineteenth centuries were expected to be itinerant evangelists as well as pastors. Broaddus's retiring disposition led him to be a school teacher, a pastor, but not an evangelist. Many road-weary pastors took note of Broaddus's example. By the middle of the nineteenth century more and more pastors cut back on their travels.

Robert Boyte Crawford Howell

R. B. C. Howell was a pioneer preacher and a complex person. Born in North Carolina, he had the refinements of a Richmond gentleman and chose to be a pioneer preacher in Tennessee. He had been a successful lawyer and pastor. From 1827 to 1834, Howell baptized 519 persons while serving as pastor of the Cumberland Street Baptist Church in Norfolk, Virginia. However, the challenge of serving the First Baptist Church of Nashville, Tennessee (which was still considered pioneer work) appealed to Howell. The church thrived under his leadership, and Howell, thinking his work in Tennessee was finished, returned to Virginia in 1850. In 1857 Howell returned to Nashville and again served First Baptist, this time until 1868.

Howell used a great deal of argumentation in his preaching. This was due as much to the controversies of the day, especially Landmarkism, as it was to his legal training. Denominational dissent brings out the best in some preachers, but not all. Fortunately, dissent brought out the best in Howell.

Jeremiah Vardeman

Jeremiah Vardeman is credited with establishing the invitation as an integral part of a Baptist sermon. If so, Vardeman initiated the practice quite innocently. Vardeman was converted in 1792 at the age of seventeen. For the next seven years Vardeman's life did not seem to show that he had been converted. For whatever reason, Vardeman attended a Sunday service in 1799. The text for the sermon was 2 Peter 2:22 and Vardeman felt that the text described him perfectly: ". . . the dog is turned to his vomit again, and the sow that was washed to her wallowing in the mire." Less than a week later Vardeman literally found himself preaching to a group of people. He recalled that he had led people toward sin and now he would give his life to leading people to Jesus. As a matter of course in his sermon, Vardeman urged the people not to wait but to change their lives immediately. He was surprised at the number of people who came forward to express sorrow for their sin. Vardeman made this invitation a regular part of his sermons.

John Mason Peck noted in a letter how Vardeman worked the invitation into his sermon.

> . . . if, at any time, he thought he could do more good, and awaken the conscience of a guilty sinner, he would break off from the regular discussion of his subject, and make a pathetic appeal to the ungodly to flee from the wrath to come.[23]

BLACK PREACHERS

Black Baptist churches also came into being during this era. The Silver Bluff Church formed in Aiken County, South Carolina, around 1775 has often been cited as the first Black Baptist church in the South. Some historical records indicate that Blacks attended church with whites in Virginia in the 1750s, but there is no concrete historical evidence of a church existing prior to the one in South Carolina. The Silver Bluff Church was founded by an itinerant preacher known to us only as *Brother Palmer.* During the Revolution, members of Silver Bluff fled to Savannah and merged with the fledgling African Baptist Church formed by former slave *George Lisle.* In order to retain his freedom, Lisle fled to Jamaica and established a church there. "Though not appointed by any board or society, Lisle was one of the earliest Baptist missionaries to go to a foreign field to preach the gospel, antedating William Carey by a decade."

---

23. Sprague, 426.

Andrew Bryan succeeded Lisle as pastor. Bryan led the church to erect a building just outside Savannah. By 1800, the church had seven hundred members.

CONClusioN

Although evangelistic preaching was prominent, preaching in the South from the 1670s to 1800 was primarily issue-centered. Among the many factors influencing the preaching of this era (and being influenced by the preaching) were those based on some form of dissent. Perhaps the primary cause of dissent in preaching was a governmental attempt to wed the church to the state. Oliver Hart and John Leland exemplified this type of preaching. For Hart, Leland, and others like them, issue-centered sermons were initially the only kind they cared to preach. To them, expository sermons were superficial and beside the point. They were not concerned with biblical details, but biblical principle, especially the biblical principal that the state would not control the church.

The slavery issue also became a dissent against the federal government and against some fellow Christians. Furman was the leader here, and some of his preaching, therefore, was issue-centered. However, Furman, in his lengthy career, also preached sermons that were Bible-centered, as well as issue-centered. Furman was known for his evangelistic and doctrinal sermons, and for his apologetic issue-centered sermons.

Doctrinal dissent between General and Particular Baptists, between Regulars and Separate Baptists led to Bible-centered preaching most of the time. Their doctrinal preaching was not motivated so much to impart information as it was to prove orthodoxy or correctness at the expense of the doctrinal stances of others.

CHAPTER 2

Establishing an Identity
(1800-1845)

The Baptists who arrived in Charles Town in the 1670s would have been pleasantly overwhelmed at the levels of prominence and social acceptance that Baptists had achieved by the early 1800s. The First Baptist Church of Charleston had become the most prestigious church in the South. The commitment of Baptists to religious liberty, evangelism, missions, and to a high view of Scripture continued to be strong. Baptists were reaping the benefits of another "Great Awakening." In addition, Baptists were held in much higher regard by society in general. No longer considered just a thorny breakaway backwoods sect, Baptists had become prominent, if not dominant, in many parts of the South. The Bullens, for example, would have been astonished to have learned that Baptist churches were so numerous that a person was never more than one day's horseback ride away from a Baptist church. Most especially, the Bullens would have been pleased to have known that their direct descendant, William Bullen Johnson, was one of the most respected Baptist preachers of the day.

Separate and Regular Baptist preachers came to realize that neither an over-emphasis on emotion, nor an over-balance on academics was desirable for preaching. Separate Baptists increasingly were absorbed into main-stream social life without sacrificing their doctrinal convictions. Educational opportunities were more available. Suspicion of formal education began to wane. More and more, Baptist preachers in the early 1800s began to seek rather than disdain education. Where college or university training was not available, preachers studied with pastors who had formal training. If an educated pastor was not available, books were, and many preachers immersed themselves in as much self-study as their resources would allow. This turn toward educational improvement did not deter, as Separate Baptists claimed it would, evangelistic zeal. Preachers like Richard Fuller and J.B. Jeter, for example, who were well educated, were noted soul-winners. The education of preachers helped rather than hindered evangelistic efforts.

Theological debates among Baptists continued into the early 1800s. The old Separate-Regular Baptist differences still existed, but were not so pronounced. The General-Particular Baptist differences still existed and were debated passionately, but other contentions arose including missions, slavery, and Landmarkism. It is interesting to note that some form of each of these Baptist differences exists today.

The sermons available to us from this era display a variety in hermeneutics and in homiletical form. One of the key issues of the day — Landmarkism — seemed to have dictated a topical approach to preaching, especially since most preachers were more interested in "proving" a point rather than preaching an exposition of Scripture text. Missionary endeavor was another key issue, and the mission sermons were usually expository in form, and strong in their biblical authority. The concern for spreading the gospel in America as well as in foreign countries was certainly genuine. The sermons preached on slavery, another key issue, only seemed expository, but in fact they often used a hermeneutic, dominated by rationalism, and by a lack of concern for historical context of the biblical passages that dealt with slavery.

The preachers of this era had the same differences of style that any era would have, ranging from the dry, almost didactic approach of Richard Furman to the flowery eloquence of Richard

Fuller. As always, the story of Southern Baptist preaching is best found in the preachers themselves. Because of the extreme importance of some of these preachers to the founding of the Southern Baptist Convention, we include lengthier digests of their sermons.

Basil Manly, Sr. (1798-1868)

Basil Manly, Sr., dreamed of formal theological education for Baptist preachers in the South. He studied theology on his own, and did a good job of it. In 1826, when he was twenty-eight years old, the First Baptist Church of Charleston, South Carolina, called Manly as their pastor. If there was any comparison by church members of Manly to Furman, who died in 1825, Manly bore it well. He served the church until 1837, when he became the president of the University of Alabama.

While in Alabama, Manly helped found the Alabama Historical Commission in 1845, and played a leading role in the organization of the Southern Baptist Convention that year. He resigned as president of the University of Alabama in 1855, but returned to Alabama in 1860 to pastor the First Baptist Church of Montgomery. Manly died in 1868 in Greenville, South Carolina, where his son Basil Manly, Jr., was a faculty member in the Southern Baptist Theological Seminary.

The only sermon by Manly available to us was preached April 8, 1849, at Pleasant Grove Church in Fayette County, Alabama. The sermon and text illustrated Manly's high view of Scripture and are closely related. Manly, however, did have a Particular Baptist theology that is obvious in the sermon. The sermon was built primarily on argumentation, with corroborating exposition. The use of application and illustration was limited, uncharacteristic for that day.

His sermon also reflects the emphasis on doctrine that characterized so much Baptist preaching until the mid-twentieth century. Manly gave careful, detailed attention to doctrine in his preaching.

Text: Philippians 2:12-13

Introduction:

He could not mean, by working out our own salvation, *devising the plan;* - that is the Father's work, and was done long ago. Not *redemption* or *justification;* - these were the Son's work, and were accomplished in that one offering, completed when he said 'it is *finished,*' and went to plead that finished sacrifice before the throne of God. Not *regeneration;* - that is the Spirit's work, and is evidently supposed to have been already wrought in those very persons; - they were saved - saints; - so far, therefore, as regards regeneration, and sanctification, (in part at least,) salvation was already wrought in them.

Body:

Commands and petitions are mingled all through the Scriptures; and, taken together, prove that men both act, and are acted upon, by *a divine operation* (italics mine). Commands prove that men act; - for, when God says *do any thing,* it implies that men are not stocks, not stones, but moral agents - capable of moral suasion, of understanding and acting, upon motives freely. Prayers, on the other hand, suppose that God acts on us, - that he both can, and will, work in us; both to will and to do. There is no man that prays, but believes that God can hear, and answer, and bless him; and that without that blessing, he is lost, darkened, blinded, sinful, - and will remain so forever. This implies that God does influence the mind by a divine operation. If we pray for the conversion of sinners, do we mean what we say? If we do, we expect God to attend the just means of grace with his blessing. In time, the fact that we do any thing in obedience and ask God's blessing in it, unites both these truths in harmony - that men freely act, and yet are acted on by a divine operation.

. . . if God knows all things, he knows who will be saved. But, could God know who will be saved, if it were not capable of being seen, as certain. But if, in order to be saved, a divine operation is necessary, and the incipient part of that operation belongs to God, could he foreknow that the man would believe, unless he had a gracious purpose to work this operation in him, so that he might believe?

1. *It grows out of this doctrine that men's actions are their own.* If faith is wrought in the heart by a divine operation, it does not hinder its being *we,* truly, that believe. If repentance is given by

Christ, it is still really *we* that repent. God may work in us to will and to do; but *we* will, *we* do. Faith is produced by His spirit in our hearts, but *we* believe. He may produce the actions; but the actions are ours. This cannot be altered or disguised.

2. *Necessity in human action is not the same as compulsion.* If God works in us to will and to do, there is a *necessity* that we should will and do; but we are not *compelled* either to will or do. The act is obliged to be; but the man, in acting, is free. He is left to act freely, and as a matter of choice. In regard to salvation, so far from compelling a man, against his will, the very thing which God does is to make him willing to act right; of his own choice, and under sufficient motive. The Christian is willing, and chooses to do right; because a divine operation has made him so. He feels free; he is conscious that he is as heartily free in now trying to serve God, as when he went after the vanities and follies of his unconverted state. He now chooses the one, as he once chose the other; and if he is obliged to refer the change of mind and heart, which produced this choice, to God, this does not mar his perfect consciousness that he is now free in choosing Christ.

3. *Sinners are free in working out their own destruction,* not withstanding the divine work on them; just as the saints are free in working out their own salvation, while God works in them to will and to do, of his good pleasure.

4. *God converts sinners in a way consistent with their moral freedom.* That it is God's work to convert a soul, let all Heaven and Earth, and every Saint, arise and proclaim.

5. *God is perfectly sincere in his counsels and invitations, notwithstanding his divine foreknowledge of the consequences.* That a God of Omniscience foresees that one person will repent, and that another will not, must be admitted by all. Yet, He offers mercy to all.

Conclusion:

. . . if men have not the grace which changes their hearts, and turns them from their sinful dispositions, have they a right to complain? I answer,

(1) They have no right to that grace; they have no claim on God for it; they are guilty, and condemned, and *deserve* nothing but woe at his hands. (2) God has promised it to them, if they wish it and seek for it. He promises, with the utmost clearness, to give his

spirit to them that ask it. Can they complain, then, if they have not that which they have not thought fit to ask, honestly and earnestly, - which they do not wish? There is no holiness in an act which is not free; and, if God were to compel you, against your will, not by moral suasion or means consentaneous to the nature of the mind, - if grace is to bring a man to the truth, without *motive,* without *his will;* then it would be without holiness: and, we learn that "without holiness no man shall see the Lord."

Manly did not paint vivid word pictures or spin homely illustrations. Manly's pulpit appeal was found in this theological depth.

William Bullein Johnson (1782-1862)

William Bullein Johnson was the obvious choice to serve as the chief architect and first president of the Southern Baptist Convention. He was a direct descendant of the first Baptists in South Carolina. He was a sharp-minded, well-educated, experienced and gentlemanly conciliator who visualized a strong, mission-minded organization of Baptists in the South. In his acceptance speech when elected president of the Triennial Convention in 1841, Johnson exemplified these qualities.

The President of this body is not called to preside over the Legislature of a Nation, or the destinies of an earthly kingdom. The affairs of such bodies relate to *time.* The deliberations of this body relate to *eternity.* The members of this body, redeemed from sin and hell, are associated together for the purpose of disseminating the blessings of eternal life to the perishing millions of the heathen world. In such an assembly there is no place for strife or vainglory. The fear of God, a singleness of eye to His honor, a regard for the spiritual and eternal welfare of man must predominate and guide the counsels, and form the decisions of its members.[1]

S.H. Ford, editor of the *Christian Repository,* attended the 1846 meeting of the Southern Baptist Convention, and reported of Johnson:

1. Quoted in Hortense Woodson, *Giant in the Land* (Nashville: Broadman Press, 1950), 98.

> To say he presides with more than common dignity, were only to repeat a well known fact. He possesses all the requisites of a good chairman, quick discernment, promptness, and decision in taking the sense of the house. . . . In his intercourse with others, (Johnson) is amiable and kind. . . . Emphatically a peace maker, he seeks every opportunity to banish discord and to promote harmony.[2]

Johnson was born at John's Island, South Carolina, June 13, 1782. He was twenty-two years old when he was converted. In January, 1805, Johnson preached at the Euhaw Baptist Church. A year later he was ordained, and served as pastor at Euhaw for a brief time. Johnson moved to Columbia, South Carolina, and by 1809 he had helped in the founding of what is now the First Baptist Church of Columbia.

In 1813, Johnson became one of many Baptists who had been persuaded by Luther Rice to new heights of missionary activity. Johnson, along with others, had seen a need for an organization of churches to focus on missionary efforts. Thus, the Triennial Convention was born in 1814.

Johnson was also active in increasing educational opportunities in the South. As president (and one of the founders) of the South Carolina Baptist Convention, he supported the founding of the Furman Baptist Academy (later, Furman University) in 1825. Also, since 1817, Johnson had dreamed of a Baptist seminary in the South.

The only sermon of Johnson's available to us was preached before the Charleston Baptist Association November 4, 1822. This sermon was built on implications rather than direct exposition of the text. The sermon is pedantic and developed strongly along the lines of Aristotelian logic, which was a prevailing style among educated preachers in the early nineteenth century. Johnson, as Manly, upheld the Particular Baptist point of view.

Text: 1 John 4:16

Title: Love Characteristic of the Deity[3]

---

2. Ibid., 132-33.

3. William B. Johnson, *Love Characteristic of the Deity* (Charleston, S.C.: W. Riley, 1823) pamphlet.

How delightful is it then to turn our attention from the scenes of earth, in which disorder and wretchedness are exhibited, up to the Great Author of universal nature, to contemplate his adorable perfections, to catch some faint views of his ever blessed nature, to mark the operations of his infinite mind; and to trace his great designs in the arrangements of his wisdom, the plans of his goodness, and the exertions of his power!

By the love of God, I shall not only understand the expression of his particular regard to individuals, but the exercise of infinite benevolence or good will to being, in general, or in other words, a supreme regard to the highest good of the universe. We begin with the exercises of this love.

I. The first exercise of this love is exhibited in the choice of that object, the accomplishment of which is the chief end of Jehovah's pursuit. This is his own glory.

Now in making his glory the chief object of his pursuit, Jehovah affords a clear proof of his nature as a God of love, or infinite benevolence. For intimately and inseparably connected with the accomplishment of this object, is the preservation of his government, and the happiness of his creatures.

II. The second exercise of divine love consists in selecting the plan which shall best secure the object proposed for its operation.

The goodness, and the wisdom employed in forming this plan, must originate in love, or infinite benevolence, with a supreme regard to the greatest good of the Universe, or being in general. This is necessarily implied in the perfections of the scheme devised. In this exercise of the Divine Mind, the nature of the Deity as a God of love is strikingly displayed.

III. The further proof and illustration of the important truth, the subject of our text will be exhibited in the consideration of those parts of the divine plan which are made known unto us.

These are: The formation of the Universe - The creation of angels and men: of the former, the preservation of an innumerable host in holiness, and the irrecoverable apostasy of fallen myriads; of the latter, the degeneracy of the whole race, and the recovery of a part - The atonement of the Lord Jesus Christ, and its glorious results.

IV. The creation of angels with the preservation of an innumerable host of them in holiness, and the permitted, irrecoverable apostasy of perverse myriads from their number, in connection with the exercise of divine justice in relation to them, afford another display of the divine glory.

V.   Another manifestation of the divine glory presents itself to our consideration in the creation of man, the degeneracy of his whole race, and the ultimate recovery of a part. In the exuberance of divine goodness, God caused a new race of beings to be formed in his own likeness, to become the recipients of his bounty, and the instruments of reflecting his glory in a more exalted degree, than had yet been presented to the universe.

It hath, notwithstanding, pleased God, to regard his apostate and helpless creatures, with the tenderest compassion, and with unbounded love. He therefore did not doom them to immediate and interminable misery, but in the exercise of unparalleled condescension and grace, provided a Mediator for them.

Having gone through the proof and illustration of the great truth contained in our text, I shall now solicit your attention to an inference or two, naturally deducible from the subject.

Inference 1. As it appears from this subject that God pursues His own glory in every thing that He does, it affords important instruction to His creatures in relation to their duty. They should make the object the chief end of their pursuits.

Inference 2. We learn further from this subject, that great encouragement should be taken in the prosecution of any plan formed on right principles, and having for its object the glory of God.

Inference 3. We learn again from this subject the duty of submission to God, of confidence in his purposes, and of composure in the confused state of the world.

God is love, or infinite benevolence. He reigns over the whole earth. He reigns in righteousness and power.

Inference 4. It appears from our subject that God has provided a costly sacrifice for the redemption of sinners. Let this amazing display of divine love teach us to make sacrifices for his service, and for the prosperity of his kingdom. . . .

Inference 5. Let this subject teach us with effect, as it is calculated to do, to love God more sincerely, more fervently, and with supreme affection; to give Him our whole hearts, and to devote ourselves with intenseness of desire, and ardency of zeal to His service, in the most unreserved manner. Let it also teach us to love our brethren; for we have received this commandment, that he who loveth God, loveth his brother also.

May we so imbibe the spirit of divine love, and so imitate the character of God, that we may stand approved in His sight, when all created things shall be eclipsed in the superior splendours of His uncreated glories.

Johnson was a teaching type preacher whose gifts for orderliness and detail were used to shape a convention of Baptists in the South.

Richard Fuller (1804-1876)

Richard Fuller was the epitome of a good Baptist preacher. He combined devotion to Scripture, zeal for missions and evangelism, and clarity in his homiletics. Born to a wealthy family, he received a good education which included a degree from Harvard. He was given much by way of advantages in life. To whom much is given, much can be expected. Fuller met those expectations.

Fuller was born April 22, 1804, in Beaufort, South Carolina, home of Beaufort College where William T. Brantly taught. He received a law degree from Harvard and was a successful attorney. On October 26, 1831, he attended a revival service at the Beaufort Baptist Church (where Brantly had pastored). Fuller marked that date in his family Bible as the day he became a Christian. Almost immediately after his baptism, the church called the twenty-seven-year-old Fuller to be its pastor. He served at Beaufort until 1847 when he left to become pastor of the Seventh Baptist Church in Baltimore, Maryland. In 1871, he became pastor of the Eutaw Place Baptist Church in Baltimore where he served until his death in 1876.

Fuller was respected as a preacher. In 1841, he preached the Triennial Baptist Convention sermon, and in 1846 he preached the first Southern Baptist Convention sermon. In 1859 and 1861, he was elected president of the Southern Baptist Convention. The Triennial Convention sermon in 1841 provided him a national reputation as an outstanding preacher. That sermon, "The Cross," reflected the deep feelings of the pastor. The sermon contained the same, timeless truths of the cross that need to be preached to every generation. The sermon, therefore, had a strong, direct relationship to its text and is representative of Fuller's high view of Scripture. The sermon was a homily (without formal outline points), and was non-polemical in style, which was unusual for that day.

Fuller spoke with more flair for feelings and emotions than Manly or Johnson. Whereas Manly and Johnson began their sermons with doctrinal pronouncements, Fuller began with an illustration. Doctrine abounded in the sermons of Fuller, but he enlivened the doctrinal sections with anecdotes and analogies. For example, note the references in the sermon which follows to the preacher or missionary possibly being a weak man whose strength is found in the cross; to the critics who disdain excitement in their Christian lives; to his own emotions.

Text: John 12:32

Title: The Cross

Introduction:

Illustration of Constantine's alleged vision of a cross in the heavens, and various illustrations from Scripture related to the cross.

Body:

Wherever a preacher or a missionary goes — he may be a weak man, an unlearned man — but he goes armed with this, and by this he will conquer. Christ "lifted up" will be an argument to do what no reasoning, no philosophy can do — an argument high as heaven, and deep as hell, and against which no sophistry of earth, no subtlety of the devil can avail. The proudest intellect will confess its conclusiveness; and the feeblest, that of the African and the untutored Burman, will rejoice in its majestic simplicity.

Whatever the heedlessness of a man, there is in the cross an energy to rouse him, a power which ever has been, and ever will be acknowledged. This is the second proposition I advanced, and one which does not appear to me to require any proof. Why, look at history; — I appeal to facts; — I appeal to the thousands of all nations, ages, sexes, temperaments, and conditions, who have confessed this energy of the cross, and yielded to it. And if there be, in all this uncounted assembly, one who has never felt anything while a bleeding Jesus has been lifted before him, then I know nothing of the human heart; let him stand up — I wish to look at him; he is more or less than man.

We have amongst us a class of people, who are always crying out — "No excitement, we do not want excitement in religion." Very well, let them get a preacher who knows nothing of Christ crucified in the heart, and says nothing of Christ crucified in the pulpit, and he will walk at their head, and lead them quietly and comfortably enough down to hell.

No brethren, the unparalleled phenomenon exhibited on Calvary, eighteen hundred years ago, can never die, can never grow old; and wheresoever that is proclaimed, there men's hearts will be shaken; the strings long silent will be swept by an unseen hand; the wells long sealed hermetically will be opened, and the waters stirred to their inmost depths.

Conclusion:

. . . the import of the term may be, and literally is, "Unite." Let us adopt this meaning, and then let, oh, let the love of Christ unite us. "Who," asks the apostle, "shall separate us from the love of God which is in Christ Jesus our Lord?" And I — I exclaim, with equal confidence, who, what, shall separate us from each other, united as we are by this love? What shall separate us? Shall persecution? No, that will only bind us closer. Shall the feuds by which in this world society is torn, and even members of the same family armed and exasperated against each other — sectional jealousies, and political rancor, and party malignity? No, the cross which lifted the Saviour from the earth, lifts us high above these petty tumults and distractions. What then? — what shall separate us? Internal strife, internal dissension? God forbid. No, my brethren, I am persuaded better things of you. No, never, never, never; it cannot be. No, by our common toils and sufferings as Baptists; by the venerable men who sang together over the cradle of this convention — those whose reverend forms I still see lingering fondly here — and those who this night, it is no presumption to believe, are beholding us with ineffable concern even from their thrones in glory; by the blood which cements us, and the new commandment written in that blood; by the memory and love of him who hath bound us together with ties indissoluble and eternal, and who is now in our midst, showing his wounds, his hands, his feet, his side, his head, and saying, "as I have loved you even so ought ye to love one another;" by all the glorious recollections of the past, and by all the more glorious anticipations of the future — this must not, will not, shall not, cannot be.

But my heart is too full. I must stop. My tears will not allow me to say many things I had wished to say. My feelings choke my utterance. Let me only repeat the Apostle's words — "The love of Christ constraineth us." Let me only renew the exhortation, Get nearer the cross. Live nearer the cross. Then no discord can interrupt our union, no troublesome birds of prey disconcert our sacrifice.[4]

No wonder this sermon brought national fame to Richard Fuller in 1841! The same sermon would have the same impact today.

Jeremiah Bell Jeter (1802-1880)

Jeremiah Bell (J.B.) Jeter so impressed Luther Rice that Rice offered to finance his college education. Jeter consulted some older minister friends who suggested that he could use his time more effectively if he would just preach and not be burdened with an education. Even as he declined Rice's offer of financial support, Jeter also declined the advice of his minister friends. He decided to pursue an education on his own terms. Jeter developed a "Paul-Timothy" relationship with Daniel Chambliss, a pastor in Sussex County, Virginia, and he began a lifelong process of self-education beginning with Chambliss' ample library.

Jeter was born in Bedford County, Virginia, in 1802. He did not grow up in a Christian home, but testified that he was deeply impressed as a youth when his mother spoke "on pious subjects."[5] Jeter struggled with conversion for years before accepting Christ in 1821. He preached his first sermon immediately after being baptized. He seemed to have had Separate Baptist spirit, but Regular Baptist organization in his sermons. In 1836 he was called as pastor of the prominent First Baptist Church of Richmond. In thirteen years and six months, Jeter baptized one thousand persons there. In 1849, he moved to the frontier and became pastor of the Second Baptist Church of St. Louis, Missouri. His supporters and detractors in St. Louis were in equal number. By 1853, Jeter returned to Richmond, this time to pastor the Grace Baptist Church. His seventeen years at Grace are considered by his biographers to have been his most productive years.

---

4. Richard Fuller, *The Cross* (Philadelphia: American Baptist Publication Society, 1841).

5. J.B. Jeter, *The Recollection of a Long Life* (Richmond: The Religious Herald Co., 1891), 4.

In 1865 Jeter and E.A. Dickinson purchased the Virginia's state Baptist paper, the *Religious Herald*. Jeter served as senior editor until his death in 1880.

Jeter did not use a byline, but several articles and many sermons published in the *Herald* were attributed to him. One of the articles was titled, "The Preparation of Sermons."[6] The article was practical, plainly written, and coincided with the teaching of rhetoric in that day.[7]

> The Preparation of Sermons
>
> So diversified are the capacities, gifts, and tastes of preachers, that no one method in preparing for the pulpit can suit them all, nor can it even suit a single preacher under all circumstances. As a general thing, extempore sermons are to be preferred to written ones. . . . First, select a text, adapted to the occasion on which it is to be used, having reference, not to its sound, but to its sense and application. Study it carefully in the light of its context, and of parallel passages. Then examine commentators or other authorities, to gain further light and to avoid falling into mistakes. Note down on a piece of paper all the thoughts that seem material, either for the elucidation or improvement of the subject, as they occur to the mind, without any reference to method. The matter for the sermon having been obtained, the next thing to be attended to is arrangement. Let this be simple as possible having, ordinarily, but few heads — not more than three or four — plainly and briefly expressed. Under these heads note down . . . so much of the matter prepared as may be needed for their explanation or enforcement, carefully excluding whatever is not relative to the point at hand. To the body of the sermon it is usually proper to append a few practical or impressive remarks.
>
> The notes are now prepared for careful and minute study. Let the preacher read them over, a paragraph at a time, committing it thoroughly to memory, and impressing his mind with what is proper to be said on that point. Throughout the time of preparation, he should seek to have the spirit of prayer, that his heart may be burdened with the importance of his theme and the responsibility of his mission. He is now ready for the pulpit. Let him aim, in the delivery of the sermon, to be calm, self-pos-

---

6. "The Preparation of Sermons," *Religious Herald*, II ns (August 22, 1867), 2.

7. The rhetoric of the day was taken largely from Plato and involved five steps: creation (sometimes called invention or finding the main idea), arrangement, style, memorization, and delivery.

sessed, and to abandon himself to the inspiration of his theme, depending on his mental activity for language, and not rejecting such thoughts or illustrations as, in the ardor of delivery may occur fresh to his mind. He should seek to be plain, pointed, earnest and brief. Should he fail, let him try again — should he succeed, let him resolve to do better next time. And let him remember, that if he would gather fruit unto eternal life, he must not only sow in the pulpit, but water by prayer in the closet.

Jeter's article, in many ways, still reads like a summary of how preaching classes are taught in Southern Baptist seminaries today.

James Robinson Graves (1820-1893)

James Robinson (J.R.) Graves's influence on Southern Baptist preaching continues today. Unfortunately, that influence was born, nurtured, and survived by means of controversy. Graves, true to the polemical style of his day, was not a man who inspired neutrality. In fact, borrowing a little from the King James style of expression, Graves was the cause of no small dispute among Southern Baptists. The controversy is known to us as "Landmarkism." The Landmark controversy has yet to be fully resolved among Southern Baptists.

Graves, born in Vermont in 1820, left the Congregationalist church to become a Baptist in 1835. He moved to Ohio in 1839. During his two years there, he was ordained as a Baptist minister and debated with Campbellites. In 1841, he moved to Kentucky to teach school and embark on a program of intensive self-study. In 1845, Graves moved to Nashville to serve as a pastor and editor of the Tennessee state Baptist newspaper. It was during his years in Tennessee that Graves began the Landmark movement.

Graves's gift for debate was reflected in his sermons which were argumentative, logically arranged, and full of rationalistic theological conclusions. As a result, his sermons were strong in clarity. Graves had a gift for developing his arguments step-by-step, seeking agreement with each isolated idea and then springing his conclusion on the congregation as if they had agreed to it all along. He also achieved what is sometimes called "image level communication," especially in his illustrations. He enabled the congregation to "see," and thus to empathize. No wonder that Graves's biographers claim that he could preach for two hours or more and the congregation would beg him not to stop. Biblical authority, however, in all of Graves's sermons available to us is weak. The text was used either as an attention sustaining slogan or as a peg on which he would hang other various highly subjective interpretations. Sermons contain little exposition of Scripture and almost no application.

Graves's personality and his communication style, commanded intense loyalty. Some people were drawn to his authoritarian stance which was the result of his dogmatism. One of Graves' favorite communication ploys was to set out some obvious biblical-historical statement early in the sermon. From his first words he had established with the congregation his own "expertise" by affirming what they knew to be true. Having established a base of "agreement" on the biblical-historical statement, Graves led his congregation to some interpretation of the statement. These brief interpretive statements seemed logical enough, at least on first hearing, for the congregation to accept them. With the congregation built into a mode of assent, Graves would then drive home his main point. The congregation was literally driven not only to agree, but to assert vocally their agreement with Graves during the sermon.

Graves was a powerful communicator. To this day, some maintain that Graves abused his communication gifts, while others are just as certain that he used them in the service of the Lord.

A synopsis of the sermon, "Satan Dethroned,"[8] illustrates J.R. Graves's preaching. The text simply supplies a vague validity for the sermon. The relationship of Scripture to sermon is weak. Points I and II, with their negative references to non-Landmark churches, reflect his Landmarkism.

> Text: John 12:31

---

8. J.R. Graves, *Satan Dethroned and other Sources by J.R. Graves,* ed. by O.L. Hailey (Chicago: Fleming H. Revell Co., 1929), 13-35.

Title: Satan Dethroned

Introduction:

Two thousand years have nearly passed since Christ was driven from the earth by the power of Satan; (stating an obvious truth) and what does the history of these twenty centuries teach us? That Satan has been dethroned and cast out, or has he maintained his cursed power? Has he yet been bound under the hatchments of the pit, or is he today everywhere triumphant? Alas, alas! There is, there can be, but one answer — the devil reigns. (The congregation is now in a mode of assent.)

Body:

I. *As the god of religious worship, being the author of all manner of religions, and the persecutor of the true.*

He was not satisfied with having slain the Prince of Peace, but he instigated a murderous, unrelenting, exterminating warfare upon all His followers, if possible, to blot them from the earth.

Three centuries convinced him [Satan] that he could not exterminate the followers of Christ by the sword, the rack, the prison, and the stake; and he resorted to the means he instituted, first, through Cain, and practiced through Balaam, and all false prophets and teachers and priests from that day to this; that is, to corrupting Christianity by changing the forms of church organization, its rites, its ordinances, its memberships and, finally, its vital and fundamental doctrines; and instigating men, religious men, too, to set up organizations, and call them the true churches of Christ, and so deceive the world, and even many of the friends of Christ, into these human counterfeits of Christ's true churches; hence, true Christianity has been almost supplanted by these. [By casting doubt on the validity of most existing churches, Graves has primed the congregation to infer that they should be certain their membership is in his church or church just like his.]

II. *But Satan reigns today triumphantly over the nations through civilized governments, through which he opposes and oppresses Christianity.*

We have seen that he is a very religious devil, having hundreds of churches where Christ had one: it is also true that he is the prince of politicians.

He has been a very fair devil in this. Those who have most fully sold themselves to him to do his will, and practice his arts, have generally succeeded to the chief places in earthly governments. All earthly governments have given their power and influence in favour of a false worship; have had state churches in their pay, and persecuted the churches of Christ.

III. *A better day.*

I turn from the dark and frightful picture of the past and, glancing along the finger of prophecy, catch a sight of the coming glory of the "age to come," when the reign of the serpent shall give place to that of the Prince of Peace.

But by the sword, by pestilence, by blood and slaughter such as this world has never witnessed, will Christ come to plead with all flesh; and the slain of the Lord will be many, till the wicked nations are subdued to external obedience to the law of Christ. It is by the might of Messiah's arm outstretched in vengeance that the armies of the beast and false prophet will be destroyed, and they be cast into the burning pit, and their governments and subjects taken possession of by Jesus Christ.

Conclusion:

This is the glorious future that awaits the earth, for which the dumb earth is now waiting and groaning; this is the hope of Christianity, the redemption and glorification of our bodies, and our exaltation to reign with Christ in His second coming and kingdom; it is the hope of every intelligent Christian who has the faith of Abraham today.

JAMES MAdisoN PENdlETON (1811-1891)

James Madison Pendleton was born November 20, 1811, in Spotsylvania County, Virginia, and named for the nation's fourth president. The Pendletons moved to Kentucky in 1812. The young Pendleton became a Christian in 1829, and was ordained to the ministry in 1831. He studied at a seminary in Hopkinsville, Kentucky. Later, he became a salaried pastor in Bowling Green, Kentucky. In 1852, Pendleton invited Graves to hold a revival in Bowling Green. It was at this time that Graves convinced Pendleton to support his Landmark beliefs. By 1854, Pendleton wrote a tract titled "An Old Landmark Re-set." Pendleton cited Proverbs 22:28, "Remove not the ancient landmark, which thy fathers have set." As a result, Pendleton was later described as the "prophet" of Landmarkism.[9]

---

9. W.W. Barnes, *The Southern Baptist Convention: 1845-1953* (Nashville: Broadman Press, 1954), 103.

On the issue of slavery Pendleton supported gradual emancipation. When the Civil War erupted, he accepted a call to pastor a church in Hamilton, Ohio. His last pastorate was in Upland, Pennsylvania. Both Ohio and Pennsylvania had strong abolitionist supporters.

During and just after the war years, Pendleton became active in the American Baptist Publication Society and in helping to found the Crozier Theological Seminary.

Several of Pendleton's sermons, preached between the 1850s and the 1880s, are available to us. These sermons were preached to congregations sympathetic to Landmarkism. The polemical approach so characteristic of Landmark preachers is not evident in the sermons available to us. The sermons are remarkably the same in their approach. He focused on a single verse as his text, found a subject in that text, and preached a topical sermon. As topical sermons go, these contained strong biblical authority. The text developed the topic rather than the other way around. The sermons were clearly organized and to the point. Pendleton must have had a gift for organization. Assuming that the sermons were not over-edited, we can conclude that he stayed on the subject from introduction to conclusion with no rambling in between. The conclusion was noted as "Remarks" at the end of each sermon. The "Remarks" were always points of application taken from the sermon.

A synopsis of two sermons provides a glimpse into what most of Pendleton's sermons were like.

> Text: Revelation 4:8
> Title: The Holiness of God
> *Introduction*:
>> God exerts an assimilating influence over us. Where the true God is worshipped, there will be conformity to his moral likeness.
>
> *Body*:
>> I.   The nature of his law illustrates the holiness of God.
>> II. His hatred of sin illustrates the holiness of God.
>> III. The indispensableness of holiness to salvation illustrates the holiness of God.
>> IV. The death of Christ illustrates the holiness of God.

Remarks:

As God is holy we should be holy.

We could have no access to God without a Mediator.[10]

Text: John 17:17

Title: Sanctification

Introduction:

Sanctification means set apart for a special purpose.

Body:

I. What is implied in sanctification?
   1. Sanctification implies crucifixion of sin.
   2. Sanctification implies the invigoration of
      Christian graces.
   3. Sanctification implies conformity to the moral
      image of God.

II. The Instrumentality of Divine Truth in Sanctification

III. Evidences of the Progress of the Work of Sanctification
   1. A deep sense of unworthiness
   2. An increasing hatred of sin

Remarks:

Does your life illustrate progress of sanctification? The unsanctified cannot be saved.[11]

Conclusion

The importance of evangelism in this era cannot be denied. However, issue-centered preaching began to dominate the homiletical scene between 1800-1845. Baptists continued to be the best sentries against incursions of the state into matters that belonged to the church, but this was no longer the dominant issue. Attacks against and defenses of slavery increased during this time. Furman died in 1825, but the influence of his preaching on slavery was felt for more than a century. Because of slavery, much of Baptist preaching in the South from 1800-1845 was issue-centered.

---

10. J.M. Pendleton, *Short Sermons on Important Subjects* (St. Louis: National Baptist Publication Society, 1859), 202-206.

11. Ibid., 195-201.

We must also acknowledge, however, the prominence of doctrinal preaching during this period just before the formation of the Southern Baptist Convention. Basil Manly, Sr., and William Bullein Johnson, both Calvinistic in their theology, did much not only to set the early identity of Southern Baptists, but also to set the tone for biblically-centered rather than issue-centered preaching for Southern Baptists.

Graves, however, revived some ancient communication principles. He knew his congregations and preached in ways that did not overestimate or underestimate their capability to receive a message. This new sensitivity toward the congregation would receive impetus a few years later from the most unlikely of sources.

CHAPTER 3

FORMING A CONVENTION
(1845-1900)

A remarkable era for Baptist preaching in the South began in 1845. With Landmarkism, continuing controversies surrounding mission methodologies, vestiges of the old Particular Baptist-General Baptist disputes, new doctrinal conflicts, and a Civil War, Baptist preaching in the South could have been overwhelmed. Instead, Baptist preaching in the South flourished, as it often has in times of dissent and extreme sordid unrest. The times called for preachers who could set aside personal ambition and self interests, preachers who had a vision of what Baptist life in the South should be. Such men were available and a watershed era in the story of Baptist preaching in the South began.

The slavery issue in America reached a bloody climax in 1865. As we have noted, Richard Furman provided the "scriptural" basis for justification of slavery. John Thornwell, in 1850, preached what Furman had taught. Slaveowners, however, had not been entirely negligent in sharing the gospel with their slaves. As we will note, John Jasper and Nelson G. Merry were slave converts who became mighty preachers.

Several new doctrinal conflicts arose in the last half of the nineteenth century. One controversy centered on biblical inspiration, and specifically on Crawford H. Toy, a professor of Old Testament at Southern Baptist Theological Seminary. Toy, who joined the seminary faculty in 1869, accepted the documentary hypothesis to explain the origin of the Old Testament. To many Baptists, Toy had rejected God as the author of all Scripture, and in 1879, Toy was forced to resign.

Another controversy revolved around the Landmark views of T.P. Crawford, a missionary to China. He decided that missionaries should be sent by local churches, rather than by a mission board. The Foreign Mission Board severed ties with Crawford in the 1890s.

A third controversy centered on M.T. Martin, who asserted that anyone who ever doubted his or her salvation was not saved. He took his assertion a step farther and claimed that no one could be a Christian who believed that a doubter was saved. Martin, therefore, saw church membership rolls as "a field white unto harvest" and preached to church members on the assumption that most of them were lost. The controversy festered primarily in Texas, where Martin was serving when the controversy began, and Mississippi, Martin's home state. The Texas convention refused to seat Martin in 1895 and 1899, and the Mississippi convention passed a resolution in 1897 condemning the doctrinal views of Martin.

The fourth controversy, the Hayden-Cranfill controversy, affected Texas Baptists more than other Southern Baptists. J.B. Cranfill owned and edited the Texas Baptist state paper, *The Baptist Standard.* S.A. Hayden owned and edited *The Texas Baptist and Herald.* Hayden opposed the work of state Baptist boards because he saw them as threats to the "sovereignty" of the local church. He was denied a seat at the 1897 and 1898 meetings of the Texas Baptist General Convention, and filed suit against various Texas Baptists. The suit was eventually settled out of court. In the meantime, in 1900, Hayden organized a new Baptist body known as The Baptist Missionary Association.

The Whitsitt controversy, however, was the major controversy of this era. In fact, it embroiled Baptists in the North as well as the South. William H. Whitsitt succeeded Broadus as president of the Southern Baptist Theological Seminary in 1895. Whitsitt wrote what proved to be a controversial article on Baptists for

Johnson's Universal Cyclopedia, published in the spring of 1886. Ten years later, Whitsitt wrote a book titled *A Question of Baptist History.* The article raised several questions. The book influenced the controversy. Whitsitt maintained that English Baptists had not practiced immersion until 1641 and implied that immersion had not become a normative practice for anyone until 1641. Landmarkists were incensed that Whitsitt wrote that the line of Baptist history does indeed go back to the New Testament, even though they admitted that on many occasions the line is invisible.

Also, Henry M. King, pastor of the First Baptist Church in Providence, Rhode Island, took issue with Whitsitt's claim that Roger Williams' baptism in 1639 was probably by sprinkling rather than by immersion.

T.T. Eaton, pastor of the Walnut Street Baptist Church in Louisville and editor of Kentucky's state Baptist paper, the *Western Recorder,* and B. H. Carroll, of whom more will be said later, led a group of Southern Baptists calling for Whitsitt's dismissal. By 1898, Whitsitt, in the interests of peace, resigned. Whitsitt's views, however, continued to be taught, not only by his successors, but eventually became the majority view in Southern Baptist life. W.W. Barnes summarized:

> there were other factors involved — personal factors — which became more apparent as the controversy became more acute. The conflict brought the fundamental questions to the attention of Baptists and clarified the atmosphere. Landmarkism won the battle, but lost the war. The Southern Seminary "lost its president, but did not lose its soul.[1]

The stories of this era also included dramatic efforts on the part of women to be more active in the convention. In 1868, Southern Baptist women held their first general meeting. Soon, women's missionary societies appeared all over the South. The Richmond, Virginia, Women's Missionary Society was first to give support to Edmonia Moon, missionary to China. The Woman's Missionary Union, which eventually became one of the

---

1. W.W. Barnes, *The Southern Baptist Convention, 1845-1953* (Nashville: Broadman Press, 1954), 138.

main arms of home and foreign mission support, was formally organized in 1888. The efforts of these gallant women kept Southern Baptists, including the preachers, keenly interested in missions and evangelism.

Southern Seminary was born in this era. The oldest and most continuously used book on homiletics was written in this era. A Black Baptist preacher reached national prominence in this era. Following are stories about the preachers who served remarkably well in what could have been a tragic era for Southern Baptists.

John H. Thornwell

Biographical information about John H. Thornwell is unavailable. He is worth noting, however, for his expansive sermon, "The Rights and Duties of Masters."[2] The sermon was preached May 26, 1850, at the dedication service of a church building "erected for the religious instruction of Negroes," and strongly reflects the slavery apologetic set forth by Richard Furman in 1822. Thornwell copiously developed his subject (the sermon is fifty-two pages long!). He opened by eliciting sympathy. This identified Thornwell with the congregation, which was comprised primarily of slave owners. Then he cited the biblical "justification" for slavery and the various benefits of slavery (including to the slaves) which affirmed what the congregation wanted to hear. Next, he visualized how many bad circumstances would arise if slavery were abolished (among other things, Communism would reign). Finally, he called on good Christians to evangelize the slaves who would not have had the opportunity to become Christians if they had not been enslaved.

The text of Thornwell's sermon was Colossians 4:1. "Masters, give unto *your* servants that which is just and equal; knowing that ye also have a Master in heaven."

The sermon began with extensive self-pitying and self-serving remarks:

---

2. John H. Thornwell, *The Rights and Duties of Masters* (Charleston, SC: Steam-power Press, 1850).

This triumph of Christian benevolence is the more illustrious, as having taken place in a community which has been warned by experience to watch with jealous care, all combinations of blacks.

... But I feel bound, in candour, to say, that, under the extraordinary pressure which has been upon us, it is a matter of astonishment and of devout thanksgiving to God, that we have been able, in the regulation of our domestick institutions, to preserve so much moderation, prudence, humanity and caution.

Thornwell prophetically spoke of a coming conflict: "What disasters it will be necessary to pass through before the nations can be taught the lessons of Providence—what lights shall be extinguished, and what horrors experienced, no human sagacity can foresee." The friend and the foe in this conflict were acutely divided:

The parties in this conflict are not merely abolitionists and slaveholders—they are atheists, socialists, communists, red republicans, jacobins, on the one side, and the friends of order and regulated freedom on the other. In one word, the world is the battle ground—Christianity and Atheism the combatants; and the progress of humanity the stake.

Thornwell, following Furman, then cited Scripture as justification for slavery.

The Apostle briefly sums up all that is incumbent, at the present crisis, upon the slaveholders of the South, in the words of the text — Masters, give unto your servants that which is just and equal, knowing that ye also have a Master in Heaven. It would be an useless waste of time to spend many words in proving, that the servants contemplated by the Apostle were slaves. Finding it impossible to deny that slavery, as an existing element of society, is actually sanctioned by Christ and His Apostles, those who would preserve some show of consistency in their veneration of the Scriptures, and their condemnation of us, resolve the conduct of the founders of Christianity into motives of prudence and considerations of policy. While they admit that the letter of the Scriptures is distinctly and unambiguously in our favour, they maintain that their spirit is against us, and that our Saviour was content to leave the destruction of whatsoever was morally wrong in the social fabric, to the slow progress of changes in individual opinions, wrought by the silent influence of religion, rather than endanger the stability of governments by sudden and disastrous revolutions.

Slavery was seen as the result of sin:

Slavery is a part of the curse which sin has introduced into the world, and stands in the same general relations to Christianity as poverty, sickness, disease or death. In other words, it is a relation which can only be conceived as taking place among fallen beings— tainted with a curse. It springs not from the nature of man as man, nor from the nature of society as such, but from the nature of man as sinful, and the nature of society as disordered.

A world without slavery meant a victory for communism.

Though they (the abolitionists) do not state the proposition in so many words, and in its naked form would probably dissent from it, yet a little attention to their reasoning puts it beyond doubt, that this is the radical assumption upon which they proceed—all men are bound to do specifically the same things. As there are obviously duties of some men, in some relations, which cannot be practiced by a slave, they infer that the institution strips him of his rights, and curtails the fair proportions of his humanity. The argument, fully and legitimately carried out, would condemn every arrangement of society, which did not secure to all its members an absolute equality of position; it is the very spirit of socialism and communism.

Thornwell concluded with words of encouragement.

Go on in this noble enterprise, until every slave in our borders shall know of Jesus and the resurrection; and the blessing of God will attend you — and turn back the tide of indignation which the public opinion of the world is endeavouring to roll upon you.

John Jasper (1812-1901)

One of the most poignant stories in Southern Baptist preaching is that of John Jasper. John was the twenty-fourth and last child born into the slave family of Philip and Tina Jasper. Philip died before his last son was born. Mrs. Jasper, inspired by the stories of John the Baptist, decided to name her child John. He was born July 4, 1812, a significant date and a significant year in American history.

John Jasper's conversion experience was a dramatic one, but anyone who knew John Jasper could have told us that his entire life was a dramatic one. Jasper became a Christian while in servitude to Sam Hardgrave, a deacon in the First Baptist Church of Richmond, Virginia. Hardgrave was among the first to hear Jasper's testimony. Hardgrave sent Jasper to tell others of what Jesus had done for him with the advice to "Fly like an angel, John!" In those days, a Black person could not become a preacher without the consent and supervision of the owner. Hardgrave gave that permission.

John eventually became pastor of the Sixth Mount Zion Baptist Church. When asked where were the first five Mount Zion Baptist churches, Jasper only grinned and admitted there were not any, but that he and his congregation just liked the name Sixth Mount Zion Baptist Church. The pastor of the Grace St. Baptist Church in Richmond, William E. Hatcher, tutored John in matters of Scripture, theology, and preaching. Once a pastor, Jasper gave most of the money he earned to the church building fund. The Sixth Mount Zion Baptist Church grew, not only in membership, but also in the number of white people who flocked to hear Jasper preach. The reading of Jasper's sermons are assurance that Jasper, indeed, did "Fly like an angel."

Jasper's sermons were eloquent and full of pathos. Most of his sermons were topical, and often they built on a rhetorical implication of a text rather than the direct meaning of the text. Jasper's hermeneutics were built on whatever his senses perceived. For instance, since the sun appears to rise and set, he preached "The Sun Do Move." In this sermon, Jasper "proves" that the earth is flat and that the sun moves around. A literal interpretation of various Bible verses (such as Num. 34:15: "The two tribes and the half tribe have received their inheritance on this side Jordan over against Jericho eastward toward the sun rising") gave Jasper all the "proof" he needed.

Jasper was a master of image level communication, that is, making people see in their minds the words he placed in their ears. By his strong use of drama and pathos, he involved the congregation in the sermon so that they could love Jesus as much as he did. We cannot overlook the fact that he had a thorough knowledge of the words of Scripture.

All of these qualities are obvious in the sermon "The Stone Cut out of the Mountain"[3]:

> Text: Daniel 2:45
>
> Introduction: It has always been one of the ways of God to set up men as the rulers of the people. What kind of bothers some of us— He don't always make it a point to put up good men. Just so, Nebuchadnezzar was appointed to be king of Babylon. He was one of these unlimited monarchs . . . he just did what he wanted to do.
>
> Body: Nebuchadnezzar had a dream that stirred him powerful. He rolled all night and did not sleep a wink. So he sent out and got the magicians and the astrologers and the sorcerers and the Chaldeans, and they were brought unto him. He told them that he had dreamed a dream that had troubled his spirit. And the Chaldeans asked him what the dream was. The king said that the dream had gone from him, and he couldn't remember it to save his soul. He told them, moreover, that they had to tell him the dream and what its meaning is, and that if they don't that he will have them cut all to pieces and turn their houses into a pile of rubble, and then he told them that if they will tell him the dream and give him an explanation he will give them nice gifs [sic] and put great honors upon them. It was too much for the Chaldeans.
>
> Then Nebuchadnezzar got high. He went on a tear and you know when a king gets mad you better get out of his way.
>
> Then Daniel told the king right to his face the thing that he had dreamed and what God meant by it.
>
> And now, my brethren, you remember Daniel told the king that the image that he saw in his dream was himsef [sic] ruling over all the other kingdoms. He told him also that that stone that was cut out of the mountain and came rolling down the craggy sides and broke in pieces the iron, the brass and the clay, that that was the kingdom of the Lord Jesus Christ. And he told him, furthermore, that the comming [sic] of the stone to be a great mountain means the growth of the kingdom of our Lord until it shall fill this world and shall triumph over all the other kingdoms. Daniel told the king that his kingdom was going to be taken from him, because he had

---

3. William E. Hatcher, *John Jasper: The Unmatched Negro Philosopher and Preacher* (Chicago: Fleming H. Revell Co., 1908), 108-120.

not feared the God of heaven, and in his folly and crimes he turned away from that God that rules in the heaven and holds the nations of the earth in the palms of His hands. He told him that the kingdom of Satan, that arch enemy of God, was going to tumble flat, because that stone cut out of the mountain would roll over Satan's dominions and crush it into flinders.

Conclusion: Ah, truly, it is a mighty stone, been rolling all these centuries, rolling today. May it roll through the kingdom of darkness and crush the enemies of God.

JAMES PETIGRU BOYCE (1827-1888)

James Petigru Boyce was the leader Southern Baptists needed in the late 1850s to accomplish a long-standing dream of a theological seminary in the South.

Boyce was born in South Carolina in 1827. His parents attended First Baptist Church of Charleston, but only his mother had membership in the church. The Boyce family was wealthy and encouraged James to attend the finest schools available. He attended Charleston College and graduated from Brown University in 1847. Boyce was converted during a revival led by Richard Fuller in Charleston in 1846. When he returned to Brown for his final year, Boyce knew he was called to be a minister. He studied under Francis Wayland at Brown and adopted much of Wayland's philosophy of education.

Boyce alternately served as an editor, pastor, and professor. He completed a master's degree at Princeton Theological Seminary before devoting the rest of his life to the founding and establishment of the Southern Baptist Theological Seminary. Dreams for a theological seminary in the South dated back to Richard Furman. Boyce spent two years raising money for the new school before it opened in 1859. Appropriately Boyce was the first chairman of the faculty, serving with John A. Broadus, Basil Manly, Jr., and William Williams. As chairman of the faculty, Boyce was the lone administrator and fundraiser. After the Civil War, Boyce and Broadus revived the seminary, and in 1877 it was relocated to Louisville, Kentucky.

Boyce's inaugural address set the philosophy of theological education for Southern Baptists to this day. The title of the address was "Three Changes in Theological Education."[4] The first change called for opening the seminary to every minister, rather than only those who had earned a college degree. Second, the seminary ought to develop an advanced program to equip students to teach, but especially to become authors. Third, the seminary should write an abstract of principles outlining a statement of belief which every professor should endorse.

Sermons by Boyce were not widely published, but a few of them are available to us. "Life and Death the Christian's Portion,"[5] a eulogy of Basil Manly, Sr., preached at Greenville, South Carolina, in 1868, is representative of Boyce's preaching.

> Text: 1 Corinthians 3:21-22
>
> Introduction: We are here to contemplate the life and death of Basil Manly, Sr. Just as life is the Christian's portion, so also is death.
>
> Body:
>
> I. Life is the especial portion of the Christian. Life means all of life as we know it. God intended life to be a blessing. For life to be a blessing we must walk in the ways of life God has given. Life does not cease with physical death.
>
> II. Death also is the Christian's portion. That is how the soul is drawn to heaven. The sting of death has been removed in salvation. Death is the doorway to eternal life.
>
> Conclusion: Death is the Christian's portion because it is a final testimony to Christ.

This sermon was built on secondary ideas from the text. Explanation of the text was employed heavily throughout the sermon, with little use of application, argumentation, or illustration. Emphasis on explanation, no doubt, was partially due to the occasion of the message. Boyce's other sermons and the few testimonies available regarding Boyce's preaching indicate that an emphasis on explanation of the text characterized all of Boyce's preaching.

---

4. James P. Boyce, *Life and Death the Christian's Portion* (New York: Sheldon & Co., 1869), 3-36.

5. Ibid.

One of Boyce's strengths as a preacher was his ability to say profound things in simple language. For example:

> The Holy Spirit dwells within the heart, sanctifying by its presence and leading on to that perfection, which it is God's purpose that he shall finally attain. There is no danger, therefore, of failure in such a life. The Divine power within secures the result. The eternal purpose of God with respect to it shall assuredly be attained.[6]

The chief significance of Boyce for preaching, however, is that he popularized the practice of centering the sermon on its biblical text. Boyce was uncomfortable with the topical preaching in Southern Baptists preaching. Southern Baptists needed someone like Boyce to demonstrate a stronger use of the Bible in preaching. He became a role model. As a result, the acceptance of a textually based sermon eventually became the norm. Topical preaching was still done, but not with the frequency of previous times.

John Albert Broadus (1827-1895)

John A. Broadus was born in Culpepper County, Virginia, on January 24, 1827. He became a Christian in 1842 or 1843, and he taught in a small private school from 1844 until 1846. There Broadus began a lifetime discipline of study. He earned two degrees from the University of Virginia by 1850. On August 12, 1850, he was ordained to the gospel ministry. Broadus alternately served as a professor and chaplain at the University of Virginia, and as pastor of the Baptist church in Charlottesville from 1851 until 1855 and 1857 to 1859. Broadus loved the pastorate and literally wrenched himself from it to join the faculty of the new Southern Baptist Theological Seminary.

After the Civil War, J.P. Boyce called the faculty together to discuss reopening the seminary. The outlook was not encouraging. After intense prayer, Broadus suggested, "Suppose we quietly agree that the seminary may die, but we will die first."[7]

---

6. Ibid., 27.
7. W.W. Barnes, *The Southern Baptist Convention, 1844-1953* (Nashville: Broadman Press, 1954), 134.

Broadus wrote the oldest, most continuously used book on homiletics in the history of Christendom. While Boyce popularized the idea of centering the sermon on a biblical text, Broadus gave practical suggestions for actually doing so. Broadus began *A Treatise on the Preparation and Delivery of Sermons* in the fall semester of 1865, at Southern Seminary. When the seminary reopened on November 1, 1865, seven students enrolled. Broadus had only one student in his homiletic class. This student was blind. Broadus carefully detailed his lectures so that the blind student could conceptualize them. Those lectures were the basis of Broadus' watershed book.

Broadus was both a preacher and a teacher. "Did Broadus practice the principles of preaching that he expounded in his book?" The answer is, "Yes, and then some." When it came to style and approaches to preaching, Broadus was as varied as Pendleton was consistent. He wrote: "Every . . . speaker should cultivate *variety* of style."[8] Several of Broadus' sermons are available for study. A direct explanation of the text was often featured in the introduction, and secondary ideas of the text usually appeared in the body of the sermon. By Broadus's definition, many of his sermons were topical, but many were a combination of expository and textual. The text for many of his sermons was a single verse, but others had longer texts.

After a strong, lengthy introduction—usually the reading of a text, some exposition of the text, announcement of the subject, and a statement of a thesis or proposition which served as a transition—Broadus developed the body in a variety of ways. Some sermons were formal homilies with no stated rhetorical outline. Most sermons had body "points." In Broadus' sermons, the number of points ranged from two to six. In his book, however, Broadus stated a strong preference for three points: "but when

---

8. John A. Broadus, *A Treatise on the Preparation and Delivery of Sermons,* ed. E.C. Dargan (New York: George H. Doran Co., 1898), 360. Such variety never interfered with Broadus's high view of Scripture as it did some preachers who thought variety means to move away from the Bible in their preaching. For a good discussion about the importance of the Bible in preaching, see his "A Catechism of Bible Teaching" in *Saved to Serve,* ed. J. B. Cranfill (Dallas: Helms Printing Co., 1941), 224-225.

it [three points] is so required, as must very frequently be the case, let us employ [three points] without hesitation."[9]

Broadus introduced to preaching the four "elements": explanation, application, argumentation, and illustration. As noted, explanation in the introduction was usually directly related to the text; in the body, the explanations related to the points of the sermon which were implied from the text. Broadus almost always used explanation, illustration, and application. When he used argumentation, it was incorporated with explanation.

The conclusions of Broadus's sermons, at least as published, were brief summaries with some application. Accordingly, in his book, Broadus emphasized that conclusions ought to be specific and concise and ought to make application. The sermon "Worship"[10] is representative of Broadus.

> Text: John 4:24
>
> Introduction: (nine paragraphs of explanation) Beautiful and wonderful it is to see how admirably our Lord led the casual conversation with a stranger so as to introduce the profoundest spiritual truths. (then brief application) The art of introducing religion into conversation is needed and is worth all of your efforts. (and finally a brief transition) I shall ask two simple questions about the worship of God.
>
> I. Why should we worship God?
>
> It is due him. It is good for us.
>
> II. How should we worship God?
>
> In a house of worship.
>
> We must have expression.
>
> Conclusion: (note the use of personal pronouns to make direct application of the sermon) We must put heart into our worship. It is our duty to worship. Others will be led to God if worship is fervent.

Broadus once preached:

> We stand upon the shoulders of the past, and rejoice in our possessions, and boast; and when we grow conceited and proud of it, we are like a little boy lifted by his father's supporting arms, and

---

9. Ibid, 287.

10. John A. Broadus, *Sermons and Addresses* (Nashville: The Sunday School Board of the Southern Baptist Convention, 1886), 1-25. Preached at the dedication of the Second Baptist Church, St. Louis, Missouri, 1879.

standing on his father's shoulders, and clapping his hands above his father's head, and saying, in childish glee, "I am taller than Papa!" A childish conclusion to be sure.[11]

Generations of preachers—Southern Baptist and many others as well—have stood and now stand on the shoulders of John A. Broadus.

Rufus Columbus Burleson (1823-1901)

Rufus C. Burleson did for Texas Baptists what J.P. Boyce and John A. Broadus did for Baptists in the South. Burleson brought his gifts for preaching and his dreams for means of educating Baptist ministers to Texas in 1848. The result was that Burleson pastored the First Baptist Church of Houston until 1851, when he became president of Baylor University. Burleson guided the school through a major split and through the difficult years of the Civil War. In 1874, Burleson accepted the position of "agent" for the Peabody Education Fund in Texas. He was one of the founders of the Texas State Teachers Association, and helped establish the University of Texas. A city just south of Fort Worth was named Burleson in honor of his many contributions to Texas life.

Burleson was born August 7, 1823, near Decatur, Alabama. He studied at Summerville University and Nashville University and was licensed to preach by the First Baptist Church of Nashville, Tennessee, in December, 1840. R.B.C. Howell was pastor at that time. Burleson graduated from Western Baptist Theological Seminary in 1847 and arrived in Texas in 1848. His varied places of service in Texas gave him opportunity to speak to a wide spectrum of Texans. W.B. Denson claims that Sam Houston accepted Christ while hearing Burleson preach.[12]

Only five of Burleson's sermons are available to us. In each of the sermons, Burleson began by coming directly to his subject. In the sermon "Family Government," Burleson said, "Impelled

---

11. Quoted by V.L. Stanfield, *Favorite Sermons of John A. Broadus* (New York: Harper and Bros. 1959), 17.

12. W.B. Denson, "Dr. Burleson as a Preacher," in *The Life and Writings of Rufus C. Burleson*, ed. Georgia J. Burleson (Georgia J. Burleson, 1901), 610.

with the burning love for young people, I discuss this subject, 'Family Government.'"[13]

This particular sermon used a multiple-passage text. The various passages were introduced as the sermon unfolded point by point. Burleson's other sermons all had an announced text at the beginning. The biblical authority in Burleson's sermon varied from direct to combination (direct and casual). He used all of the functional elements abundantly, especially illustrative material. Burleson's quality education is reflected in his use of illustrative material ranging from Scripture, to literature and history, to personal experiences. In fact, Burleson was a master illustrator. During the explanation portion of his sermons, Burleson used illustrations that appealed to the intellect—literature and history—and during the application portions of the sermon, Burleson used more emotional application.

Burleson's sermon "Deaconship"[14] is reviewed here as an example of his preaching. With only five sermons available, it is difficult to say if it is typical or even representative of his preaching.

> Text: Acts 6:1-8, 1 Timothy 3:8-15. Focal passage 1 Timothy 3:13.
>
> Introduction: The deacon has important and specific responsibilities. Baptist history illustrates this. Deacon Wm. Kiffin prepared the way for Spurgeon. Deacon John D. Rockefeller has given Chicago the greatest Baptist college in the world. Deacon Levering helped Richard Fuller in Baltimore. During my more than fifty years of ministry in Texas, where I have found faithful deacons, I have found the Baptist cause prospering.
>
> I. What is the office of deacon? (Acts 6:1-8)
>
> The office was established to free preachers to give themselves to prayer and to ministry of the word. Deacons were not meant to be preachers, although some, like Stephen, became preachers after they became deacons.
>
> II. The Importance of the office (Acts 6:8; 1 Timothy 3:13)
>
> As soon as deacons were appointed we have the report that the Word increased. Wherever deacons serve well, the cause of Christ prospers. We should have a school or seminary specifically for the training of deacons.

---

13. Ibid., 613.
14. Ibid., 651-658.

III. How can we use the office of deacon well? (1 Timothy 3:8-12)

    The men called to be deacons must be Scripturally qualified. Deacons should not be the disciplinary arm of the church. The deacons should meet their Scriptural responsibilities and should promote harmony.

    Conclusion: Every member of the church should assist deacons in their ministry, and thus acting will attain great power with God in the salvation of the world.

Burleson's sermons were preached in a clear, simple, and profound style. His popularity seems to have been based on his ability to have something to say to every member of his congregation no matter their station in life.

JaMES BoARdMAN HAwThoRNE (1837-1910)

James Boardman (J.B.) Hawthorne was born in Wilcox County, Alabama, May 16, 1837. His father was a Baptist minister who claimed to have baptized between five and six thousand people in Alabama. In many ways, J.B. had a checkered career. Besides preaching, Hawthorne practiced law, served as a Confederate soldier, a Confederate chaplain, lecturer, and denominational leader. After earning two degrees from Howard University, Hawthorne was ordained in 1859. He pastored Second Baptist Church in Mobile, Alabama; First Baptist, Selma, Alabama; Franklin Square Baptist, Baltimore, Maryland; First Baptist, Albany, New York; Broadway Baptist, Louisville, Kentucky; Tabernacle Baptist, New York City; First Baptist, Montgomery, Alabama; First Baptist, Richmond, Virginia; First Baptist, Atlanta, Georgia; First Baptist, Nashville, Tennessee; and Grace Avenue Baptist, Richmond, Virginia.

Hawthorne also served as president of the Board of Education of the Alabama State Convention, corresponding editor of the *Alabama Baptist,* member of the Home Mission Board, and was one of the early advocates of a Sunday School Board to provide literature for Southern Baptist churches.

J.B. Hawthorne's strengths and weaknesses as a preacher were obvious. His contributions to Southern Baptist life were many. Hawthorne was a gifted orator. In fact Hawthorne was enamored with oratory. He so thoroughly studied the world's great orators that he was asked to lecture on the subject. He wrote that he spent hours and sometimes days writing a sermon.[15] Consequently, Hawthorne testified that even though he carried a manuscript to the pulpit, he seldom felt a need to look at it while preaching.

Hawthorne generally used one verse or less as the biblical text for his sermons. Most of the sermons are topical. The sermons range from preaching the direct ideas of the text on a few occasions, secondary ideas of the text frequently, and minor ideas in the text much of the time. Hawthorne's sermons are strong on explanation, and strong, even powerful, in application. Hawthorne used illustrations profusely, at times as many as five to seven illustrations consecutively. He used argumentation sparingly.

Due to his intensive study of oratory, Hawthorne preferred formal homilies but also used rhetorical outlines on occasion. This was a major strength in his preaching. Rather than having points, he emphasized the *point* of his sermon. Hawthorne would take the one central, key idea of the sermon and focus on it from the first sentence of the introduction to the last sentence of the conclusion. He did not ramble. Most of his sermons were strongly Christological.

Rather than presenting a sermon synopsis, as we have with other preachers, three excerpts will provide the insight we need into Hawthorne's preaching. The first two excerpts are from the sermon "An Unshaken Trust." The first excerpt illustrates his eloquence.

> From the birth of true religion to this hour, Satan, speaking through human lips, has charged that men who worship God are inspired with no higher motive than the desire of temporal aggrandizement; and though the contradiction has been made by millions of holy men who preserved their moral and religious integrity in the depths of poverty, amid the gloom of the dungeon and the flames of the stake, the lie still lives and men still repeat it with all the malignity and venom of their Satanic master.[16]

---

15. J.B. Hawthorne, *An Unshaken Trust and other Sermons* (Philadelphia: American Baptist Publication Society, 1899), 10.

16. Ibid., 29-30.

The second excerpt is an example of Hawthorne's possible overuse of illustrative material that emphasizes tragedy and borders on emotionalism:

> Go with me to yonder city of the dead. There beneath a weeping willow a mother kneels at the grave of her only child. Sorrow has plowed deep furrows on her face, but the light of hope is in her eye. As her tears fall and mingle with the dust we hear her say: "The Lord gave, the Lord hath taken away; blessed be the name of the Lord."[17]

The third excerpt is an example of Hawthorne's powerful use of direct application. This excerpt is from the sermon, "Final Reward".

> My friend, what are you? Are you a faithful servant or an idler? You may be the busiest of men in secular pursuits; you may be a merchant burdened with all the cares and complications of an extensive trade, or you may be a lawyer engaged in the most extensive practice; but if your secular vocation is divorced from religion and you are doing nothing to advance God's kingdom of truth and righteousness, you are an idler, an unprofitable servant whose reward will be an eternal heritage of shame and anguish.[18]

Hawthorne combined evangelistic zeal with his inherent gift for oratory to become an eloquent preacher.

Bεɴaȷaʜ Haʀvεy Caʀʀoll (1843-1914)

Benajah Harvey (B.H.) Carroll once entered a Civil War battlefield in Mansfield, Louisiana, seeking death. He was carried off the battlefield with a rifle ball in one of his legs and a brilliant life of ministry in his future. Carroll was born in Carroll County, Mississippi, December 12, 1843. Fifteen years later, the Carroll family moved to Burleson County, Texas. In 1859, Carroll entered Baylor University (then located at Independence, Texas). The Civil War years were troubled and unhappy years for Carroll because of severe personal problems. Shortly after the war ended, however, he accepted Jesus as his Lord and Savior at a Methodist camp meeting. In 1866, Carroll was ordained. Four years

---

17. Ibid., 34.
18. Ibid., 82-83.

later he became assistant pastor of First Baptist Church, Waco, and in 1871, he became the pastor. Carroll involved himself in many denominational activities, but his mightiest work was the founding of Southwestern Baptist Theological Seminary.

Carroll first shared his dream of a seminary in the Southwest with the Baylor trustees in 1905. He described a vision he had while riding on a train from West Texas back to Waco:

> I saw multitudes of our preachers with very limited education, with few books and with small skill in using to the best advantage even the books they had. They are consecrated men, many of them vainly hungering for better training in the work to which God has called them and to which with singular self-sacrifice they have dedicated their lives. I saw here in the Southwest many institutions for the professional training of the young teacher, the young lawyer, the young doctor, the young nurse and the young farmer, but not a single institution dedicated to the specific training of the young Baptist preacher. It weighed upon my soul like the earth on the shoulders of Atlas.[19]

His dream came true in a mighty way! Southwestern Baptist Theological Seminary was born in 1908. Carroll was its first president and served in that capacity until his death November 11, 1914.

Carroll held a high view of preaching. He expostulated his views to the Baptist General Convention of Texas October 7, 1892: "Not long ago I said to a beautiful and brilliant wife that her husband had descended when he left the pulpit just to be a governor."[20] And of the value of sermons, Carroll preached: "Just think of it seriously. Eternal interests hinge on every sermon. Every sentence may be freighted with eternal weal or woe. Every word may be the savor of life unto life or death unto death."[21]

Carroll's high view of preaching was predicated on a high view of Scripture. While preaching from 2 Timothy 3:17, Carroll said:

19. Jeff D. Ray, *B.H. Carroll* (Nashville: Sunday School Board of the Southern Baptist Convention, 1927), 136-37.

20. B.H. Carroll, *Jesus the Christ,* ed. J.B. Cranfill (Nashville: Baird-Ward Press, 1937), 210.

21. Ibid., 205.

> I certainly understand the passage to teach the plenary inspiration of the Holy Scriptures—the Old Testament directly, the New Testament by implication. That, being inspired, they are authoritative and inerrant. That as such they constitute an all sufficient standard of human belief, conduct, and destiny.[22]

Carroll preached primarily expository sermons which were often based on multiple-passage texts. Robert J. Robinson studied each of the 241 Carroll sermons available to us. Robinson concluded that 157 sermons were expository, 55 were topical, and 24 were textual.[23] Most of the sermons have direct biblical authority. Explanation was used more than the other functional elements, but there was no lack of application, argumentation, or illustration. In most instances, Carroll used a polemical style.

The intensity of Carroll's preaching virtually overwhelmed some people:

> I had the greatest difficulty in adjusting to the numerous Scriptures he always read. His deliberation weighed heavily on me at first. I wanted faster movement; notwithstanding the reward always came to anyone who listened and waited. When the sermon was over occasionally I found myself positively tired from mental strain.[24]

The introductions to Carroll's sermons usually contained a study of the historical background of the text. For example, in the introduction to "God's Measureless Power in Christian Work," Carroll said, "That you may understand this case, let us look somewhat into its history."[25] Carroll introduced the theme or subject of his sermons with succinct phrases such as, "My theme today is . . .", "The sum of this text is to show us . . .", "The object of this text is to . . .", "It is my purpose today to . . ." Carroll did not spend much time establishing rapport with the congregation.

22. B.H. Carroll, *Saved to Serve*, ed. J.B. Cranfill (Dallas: Helms Printing Co., 1941), 16.

23. Robert J. Robinson, "The Homiletical Method of Benajah Harvey Carroll" (Unpublished Th.D. dissertation, Southwestern Baptist Theological Seminary, 1956), 147-151.

24. J.M. Dawson, "B.H. Carroll as Interpreter of the Holy Scriptures," Founders Day Address (Southwestern Baptist Theological Seminary, March 14, 1952), 2-3. (Typewritten.)

25. Carroll, *Saved to Serve*, 126.

Perhaps Carroll had already related to the people outside the pulpit so thoroughly that he felt he could go straight to the exposition of the text.

Carroll used both rhetorical outlines and formal homilies in the bodies of his sermons. For example, when the text called for an outline, Carroll would use one; when it did not have obvious divisions, Carroll was comfortable with using the homily approach. The sermon "The Transfiguration"[26] had a terse outline:

    I. The Occasion

   II. The Event

  III. The Design

  IV. Its Relations

To conclude his sermons, Carroll most often used direct application. (He also used a summary of the sermon in his conclusions, and frequently quoted poetry.) Direct appeal was used, for example, in the sermon "God's Punishment of the Wicked:"[27]

> O sinner, sinner, sinner! God or the devil! Christ or Satan! . . . how can you hesitate? How can you take a moment to limp around between two opinions?
>
> The only way to find pardon for past offenses is in Christ. Will you come to Him?
>
> Here now, press through this throng — make a way — come up here now and let us unite our prayers that God today will give you the Holy Spirit that you may be led to repentance toward Him and faith in the Lord Jesus Christ.

Carroll's preaching combined a strong, direct, authoritative use of Scripture with a warm disposition toward the people to whom he preached. Both qualities are essential for effective preaching.

OTHER PREACHERS

GEORGE AUGUST LOFTON

George August Lofton was considered to be one of the outstanding theologians among Southern Baptist preachers. He

26. Carroll, *The Day of the Lord* ed. J.B. Cranfill (Nashville: Broadman Press, 1936), 154-174.

27. Ibid., 90-103.

was a defender of Whitsitt, and his book *The English Baptist Reformation,* was born out of that controversy.

Lofton was born Christmas, 1839, in Panala County, Mississippi. He pastored the Central Baptist Church in Nashville, Tennessee, from 1888 until his death December 11, 1914.

Not surprisingly, most of Lofton's sermons were expository, with a doctrinal objective. In an 1895 article in the *Baptist and Reflector,* Lofton shared three rules he always followed in sermon preparation:

1. Determine which theme will be appropriate to discuss before the congregation.

2. Analyze the text and subject in connection with the context, and then clothe the analysis with all the material of which thought and feeling are capable.

3. Write out half of the substance of the sermon, leaving the other half to be filled off hand.

Lansing Burrows

Lansing Burrows loved statistics and collected reams of information from Baptist churches. Porter Routh wrote, "[Burrows] will be remembered best . . . for his pioneering in the collection of data from Southern Baptist churches and for his thirty-two years service as senior secretary of the convention."[28]

Burrows was born in Philadelphia, Pennsylvania, April 10, 1843. His father, John, was pastor of First Baptist Church, Richmond, Virginia, for many years. Lansing was taken prisoner during the Civil War. After being released and returning home, he had an active ministry covering half a century, including eight different pastorates.

A few of Burrows' sermons were published in Baptist periodicals. Those sermons were clearly outlined and written in oratorical style. For example, in the introduction to "The Knowledge of God" from Philippians 3:10, Burrows preached:

> When I trace the handiwork of God in smiling landscapes, or in
> the scintillating heavens; or regard his power in the fury of tem-

---

28. Porter Routh, "Lansing Burrows," *The Baptist Training Union Magazine* (December, 1949), 3.

pests of the silent marshalling of worlds; or contemplate his gentleness in his care of wounded sparrows; or reflect upon his illimitable resource in the luxurious purveying of his providence, I may know much about him, and yet be a stranger to him and forbidden his presence. . . .

The outline for that sermon contained four points, developed in topical style:

I. To know Christ is to comprehend God

II. To know Christ is to apprehend Truth

III. To know Christ is to understand self

IV To know Christ is eternal Life[29]

William Eldridge Hatcher

William Eldridge Hatcher was noted for his use of humor in his preaching. When a young preacher asked him if he had yet preached his best sermon, Hatcher responded for all of us when he said, "No, but I have preached my worst one."

He was born in Bedford County, Virginia, July 25, 1844. His most notable pastorate was at Grace Street Baptist Church in Richmond, Virginia, from 1875 to 1901.

Hatcher was especially adept at preaching on Bible characters. For example, in a sermon from Matthew 12:43-44, he described the poor widow who gave her mite in offering.

> Little did that woman know that Jesus Christ was going to turn his camera upon her to get her photograph and hang it in the gallery of the elect. Little did she know that the splendor of this gift would eclipse every gift that was given that day, and little did she ever dream that the gift would go through the world telling its blessed story . . . and leading thousands of others to give.[30]

Thomas Treadwell Eaton

One never needed to ask Thomas Treadwell Eaton his views on any subject related to theology. As a prominent pastor and

29. Lansing Burrows, "The Knowledge of God," *The Tennessee Baptist* (May 24, 1884), 1-2.

30. William E. Hatcher, "Thanksgiving Sermon," *Baptist and Reflector* (January 3, 1895), 2-3.

long time editor of the *Western Recorder* in Kentucky, Eaton was a strong spokesman on every issue.

> He had his opinion of almost every question which met him, and whether in parlor, or train, or public assembly, he was ready to propose, advocate or antagonize, as seemed the fitting thing with him. His opinions were public property, spontaneously expressed and fearlessly maintained.[31]

Eaton was born in Murfreesboro, Tennessee, November 16, 1845. His father, Joseph, pastored the First Baptist Church of Murfreesboro, and simultaneously served as president of Union University. His fourth and last pastorate was at the Walnut Street Baptist Church in Louisville, Kentucky, from 1881 until his death in 1907. In Louisville, Eaton worked successfully for the resignation of W.H. Whitsitt as president of Southern Seminary.

Eaton was primarily an evangelistic preacher. A.C. Dixon wrote:

> Dr. T.T. Eaton was not only evangelical in theology; he was evangelistic in spirit. He was not content with merely edifying the saints; but, like his Master, he was ever intent upon seeking and saving the lost.[32]

Nelson G. Merry

From the time of his conversion in the fall of 1845, Nelson G. Merry felt called to preach. Merry was about twenty years old at the time. The membership book of the First Baptist Church of Nashville, Tennessee, contains this simple notation: November 9, 1845 "Nelson (Free Col'd man) Baptism." The pastor, R.B.C. Howell, regularly conducted church services for African Americans on Sunday afternoons and one night during the week. Howell took an interest in Merry and offered him some theological instruction.

Merry was licensed to preach in March, 1853. Several months later, he was called as pastor of a mission sponsored by the First Baptist Church. (The first Black minister to be ordained in Ten-

---

31. W.E. Hatcher, "Editorial," *The Baptist Argus,* July 11, 1907, 16.
32. Ibid.

nessee was Edmund Kelly. Kelly served the first Black Baptist church in Tennessee, the Mt. Lebanon Church in Columbia.)

Merry served effectively. By 1861, the church membership grew from 100 to 241. In 1870, the church membership climbed to 788. Just before his death in 1884, the church reported 2,681 active members.

Merry had a keen mind and pursued every available educational opportunity. He grasped theology quickly, and communicated effectively. White and Black Baptists spoke of his eloquence, his sensitivity to his congregation, and his oral ability in expressing various emotions. Merry died in 1884, but several churches in Tennessee credit their origin to his influence.

Conclusion

Southern Baptist preaching from 1845 to 1900 added a new element. In addition to issue-centered preaching and doctrinal preaching, Southern Baptist preaching began to be congregation-oriented. Thornwell would make one of the last great pleas for the sanctity of slavery during this era. That issue would be subsumed in justification for secession, for war, and for some explanation as to why the South was defeated in the war. Doctrinal preaching was also still important. Eaton and others became the first watchdogs for orthodoxy in the budding Southern Baptist institutions.

The new element—congregational orientation—came primarily through the influence of John Jasper and Nelson Merry. Their ability to paint word pictures and to relate Scripture to everyday experiences had tremendous appeal. As a result, Southern Baptist preachers began to think more earnestly about how their messages were being received. They thought of how the sermon would live in the hearts of their listeners long after the preaching had occurred.

The evangelistic preaching of Carroll and Burleson would combine their exegetical skills with a strong sensitivity to the capabilities of their congregations. Thus, expository preaching became more appealing to Southern Baptists during this time period.

CHAPTER 4

THE TESTING TIME
(1900-1945)

Baptists in the South between 1900 and 1945 reaffirmed their historic stances on the unique authority of Scripture, on the deity of Christ, and on the need for strong evangelistic outreach. These reaffirmations came, in part, as reactions to the liberalism and the Social Gospel movement that many other churches in America had adopted. Liberalism in those days attempted to apply scientific methodology to Scripture. As a result, liberalism generally disregarded miracles and the supernatural in general. Liberals exalted the humanity of Jesus at the expense of the deity of Jesus. Christ's pre-existence, His virgin birth, John's reference to Him as the *logos* were dismissed as "unscientific." Liberals felt liberty to rewrite, reorganize, and re-evaluate the Bible. Any notion of divine inspiration of Scripture was rejected. These theological conclusions were red flags to Baptists in general. Some Baptists reacted more strongly than others.

Fundamentalism arose as an opposite and equal reaction to liberalism. Beginning in 1910, the Bible Institute of Los Angeles, California, published *The Fundamentals: A Testimony of the Truth*. Five fundamental beliefs were outlined: (1) the inerrancy and infallibility of the Bible, (2) the virgin birth and deity of Christ, (3) the literal physical resurrection of Jesus from the dead, (4) the atoning death of Jesus as sacrifice for the sins of the world, and (5) the imminent second coming of Jesus to set up His kingdom and to reign on earth for a thousand years. Many Baptists agreed with all or some of the theological tenets of fundamentalism. Most Baptists, however, detested the militant polemics of fundamentalists. From that day to this day, many Baptists agree with fundamentalism theologically while rejecting the harsh, sometimes paranoid spirit that has infested fundamentalism.

The forces of liberalism and fundamentalism met on legal turf in Dayton, Tennessee, in 1925. The famous Scopes trial became one of the most sensational events of the 1920s. John Thomas Scopes was found guilty of disobeying a Tennessee state law by teaching the theory of evolution in a public school. The fundamentalists won the court battle, but, for the time being at least, lost the war. After the trial, American society continued to drift toward liberal theological, social, and political views.

The Social Gospel movement was popularized by Walter Rauschenbusch, a Baptist professor in the Rochester Theological Seminary. This movement was, and is, a powerful influence on American Christianity. Correctly or incorrectly, many Baptists in the South perceived that the Social Gospel movement taught that salvation came about by improving society in general, rather than by an individual professing faith in Jesus as Lord and Savior. Baptists in the South predictably and thoroughly rejected any movement that seemed to say that the work of Christ was unnecessary.

Southern Baptists in particular were also preoccupied with all of these divisive issues. In 1924, the Southern Baptist Convention appointed a committee to write a statement of faith to be presented to the 1925 convention meeting in Memphis, Tennessee. The statement included this sentence pertaining to evolution: "Man was created by the special act of God, as recorded in Genesis."[1] C.P. Stealey, editor of the Oklahoma state Baptist paper, *Baptist Messenger,* was outraged. Stealey was convinced that Southern Baptists wanted a much stronger statement. Immediately, he offered this amendment, "We believe that man

---

1. *Annual,* Southern Baptist Convention (1925), 72.

came into this world by direct creation of God and not by evolution."[2] E.Y. Mullins, offended by Stealey's amendment, and probably by his attitude as well, spoke against the amendment. The amendment was defeated 2,013 to 950.[3]

Stealey and J. Frank Norris, pastor of the First Baptist Church of Fort Worth, continued to agitate for a stronger statement against evolution in the 1926 convention. George W. McDaniel, re-elected president of the convention, included in his acceptance speech a statement rejecting "every theory, evolution or other, which teaches that man originated in, or came by way of, a lower animal ancestry." This view was adopted by the 1926 convention.

Faced with a continuing need for additional organization, the first executive committee of the Southern Baptist Convention came into being in 1917. The convention had long been troubled with financial problems; therefore, the executive committee was created to bring more efficiency in disbursing funds in hopes of alleviating convention indebtedness. The new committee endorsed an overly ambitious 75 million campaign, but it fell $17 million short of its goal. Even so, the campaign forced Southern Baptists to focus their prayers and concerns on convention indebtedness. In 1924, a committee related to the $75 million campaign called for a simultaneous every-member canvass to be held November 30 to December 7, 1924. Southern Baptist churches were urged to adopt week-by-week giving instead of the traditional semiannual financial campaigns designated vaguely for the benevolent work of the convention. In 1925, this committee recommended to the convention a "Cooperative Program" for Southern Baptists. The motion called for churches to send a portion of their offerings to their state conventions. The state conventions retained a portion of the funds and sent the rest to the executive committee in Nashville. The committee, consisting of representatives from each state including laymen and representatives from Woman's Missionary Union organizations, developed a budget for sustaining the

2. Ibid., 76.
3. Ibid.

agencies of the convention subject to the approval of the convention. The Cooperative Program became a boon to Southern Baptist life.

Several other factors influenced, or were influenced by, Southern Baptist preaching during this period. Radio programs became a staple of American life. The First Baptist Church of Shreveport, Louisiana, and its pastor, M.E. Dodd, were forerunners in broadcasting for Baptists. Racial conflicts continued to divide and even embarrass Southern Baptists. Participation in two world wars touched every Southern Baptist church. Following is a glimpse of the preachers and the preaching of Southern Baptists during the years 1900 through 1945.

GEORGE WASHINGTON TRUETT (1867-1944)

George W. Truett was born in Haynesville, North Carolina, May 6, 1867. His family moved to Whitewright, Texas, in 1889. After Truett's ordination, his pastor, R.F. Jenkins, wrote to the president of Baylor University recommending that Truett be hired as a fundraiser for the school. Jenkins wrote: "My dear Dr. Carroll. . . . There is one thing I do know about George W. Truett—whenever he speaks, the people do what he asks them to do."[4] Truett spent twenty-three months raising enough money for Baylor University to pay a burdensome $92,000 debt. He demonstrated to Texans that he was a spiritually committed, industrious, energetic, and persuasive servant of God.

Truett at first objected, but then submitted, to a call for his ordination to the gospel ministry. After Truett had lived in Whitewright, about a year, the Whitewright Baptist Church called a special business meeting in 1890. A motion by one of the members called for Truett's ordination. While Truett objected, the motion was seconded. Truett's objections began to abate as he realized that God had truly called him to preach.

Truett enrolled at Baylor in 1893. As a student, he pastored the East Waco Baptist Church. In the fall of 1897, he accepted the call to pastor the First Baptist Church of Dallas. He served

---

4. Powhatan W. James, *George W. Truett* (Nashville: Broadman Press, 1939), 52.

in that position until his death in July 1944. Truett served three terms as president of the Southern Baptist Convention beginning in 1927. He also presided over three sessions of the Baptist World Alliance. Truett was in constant demand for revivals. In 1937, during his fortieth anniversary in Dallas, Truett testified that he averaged preaching once a day during those forty years.

Some of Truett's sermons were recorded on primitive wire recording machines. The frequency response of these recordings was such that his voice sounds high-pitched, but according to those who heard Truett, he had a deep and powerful voice. On one occasion, he spoke on the steps of the Lincoln Memorial; his biographers are confident that 15,000 people heard Truett clearly and without electronic amplification.

Truett's sermons were closely tied to a biblical text, but he was not an expository preacher. He used the central idea of the text and built a textual or topical sermon around that idea. His original sermon notes are housed in the Archives section of Roberts Library of Southwestern Baptist Theological Seminary. Most of his sermon notes are not dated. Judging from any references to contemporary events, it appears that Truett made extensive notes in his early sermons. Later, brief sermon notes were written on the backs of envelopes and scraps of paper. Truett studied daily in preparing his sermons and expanded his library at every opportunity:

> Truett's study was at home, and it was filled to overflowing with his great library. He referred to his books as his tools, and spared no expense to have the best. Twice he had to build an extension to the downstairs room which served as a library-study. Shelves lined the walls, and finally filled the entire room, equipped with rolling ladders as a regular library. Carpenters came periodically to build extra shelves. Truett was a rapid and insatiable reader, gathering information, illustrations, and ideas for his many sermons and addresses.[5]

In a conversation with his personal physician, Truett declared:

5. Leon McBeth, *The First Baptist Church of Dallas: Centennial History (1869-1968)* (Grand Rapids: Zondervan, 1968), 193.

> . . . these books are my tools, and I must work. I must work long
> and hard to feed the people. Some say that Truett is brilliant, but it
> is not so. I am but a very ordinary man, and I must study long and
> hard to feed my flock.[6]

Truett maintained close contact with his flock. He received
sermon ideas from a devotional study of Scripture and from his
visits with members of his congregation which is reflected in his
unpublished sermon notes. Note the practical emphasis in his
sermon on bread:

> Text: Matthew 6:11; Luke 11:15
>
> Title: Our Daily Bread
>
> Introduction: By bread is meant the kingdom of God. This
> makes Christianity seem impractical. But Jesus is the most practi-
> cal teacher in the world. Bread is the motor power for humanity's
> industries. What drives the ploughs, spindles, ships, rigs? Bread.
>
> I.   The need for bread teaches absolute dependence on God.
> II. Teaches simplicity in our requests.
> III. Teaches the trustworthiness of God.
> IV. Teaches the lesson of Brotherhood.

Part IV served as a conclusion to the sermon.

Truett did not use explanation extensively. Consequently,
most of his sermons had secondary and casual biblical authority.
Application in Truett's sermons is extensive, strong, and direct,
with frequent use of first and second person pronouns.

Illustrations abound in Truett's sermons. The Bible and biog-
raphies were frequent sources of illustrative material for Truett.
He used hymns, current events, various figures of speech, and
occasional references to people who are identified in his hand-
written notes only by their initials. For example: "Tho' had
wealth, Mr. R. & Mr. C. are dependent as paupers," and "Mr. V.
Smith's old man and water." Truett rarely used argumentation
in his preaching. In all of his sermons and speeches he seemed
to reject any hint of polemics. In fact, Truett, as a role model for
numerous preachers, introduced an era of Southern Baptist
preaching in which argumentation would rarely be used.

---

6. *Ibid.*, 194.

EdGAR YOUNG MullINS (1860-1928)

Four major influences shaped the first half of Edgar Young (E.Y.) Mullins's adult life to prepare him for the outstanding contributions he made during the second half of his adult life. First, Mullins's father was a preacher and teacher when E.Y. was born January 5, 1860, in Franklin County, Mississippi. Late in 1867, the Mullinses moved to Corsicana, Texas, where the elder Mullins became the first pastor of First Baptist Church. Mullins was baptized there by his father in 1881. E.Y. benefited not only from his father's example but also his parents' prayers. When he was thirty-five years old, he learned that his parents had dedicated him to the ministry when he was born.

Second, Mullins benefited from the deep interests and obvious talent of his wife, who helped him evaluate his sermons.

> Frequently, he and Mrs. Mullins would analyze and criticize his sermons and addresses, especially with reference to his use of illustrations. Two artistic souls shared in the labor . . . that produced the sermons that many called master-pieces in homiletical art.[7]

The third major influence that shaped Mullins was his third pastorate. In 1895, he accepted a call to the Newton Centre Baptist Church in affluent Newton Centre, Massachusetts. A sizable population of the members of the Newton Centre Church had graduated from either Harvard, Brown, or Yale Universities. Mullins felt compelled to build his theological acumen and to structure his sermons as painstakingly as possible so as to communicate with his highly educated congregation. The result was that Mullins's sermons are models of simple, plainspoken use of language that stayed with one central objective.

Fourth, Mullins was influenced by the nineteenth-century theologian Friedrich Schleiermacher, who emphasized the importance of the individual's self-consciousness looking to Christ as the only true mediator between us and God.[8]

---

7. Harold W. Tribble, "E.Y. Mullins," *Review and Expositor,* 49 (April 1952), 135.
8. The title of Mullins's theological system, *The Christian Religion in Its Doctrinal Expression,* reflects Schleiermacher's influence.

In 1899, Mullins became president of Southern Seminary. As president, he also taught courses in theology. The investment of study and practice of ministry in the first half of his adult life paid dividends. His dedication to God, excellent administrative skill, theological incisiveness, and homiletical efficiency marked Mullins as one of Southern Baptists' finest models of humility.

Most of Mullins's sermons, predictably, were doctrinal and had direct biblical authority. Typical of Mullins's preaching was his sermon "The Lordship of Christ." The influence of Schleiermacher appears most specifically in the first subprint under major point II.

> Text: Acts 2:36
>
> Introduction: The experience of the disciples was like a new creation. Notice two parallels in this new creation: the Lordship of Christ becomes more and more absolute, and the might of the church grows in splendor.
>
> I propose to define what are the sources of Christ's Lordship and what is the relationship between the Lordship of Christ and the conquest of the world by the church.
>
> I. The ground of Christ's Lordship ("God hath made him both Lord and Christ whom you crucified")
>
> > Jesus is Lord through divine appointment. Jesus is Lord through suffering. The Lordship of Christ is based on what He did. Not a teaching, but an event is the cornerstone of his Lordship.
>
> II. The Method of Christ's Lordship. Three paradoxes.
>
> > 1. Jesus' authoritative revelations of truth are designed to lead to human discoveries of truth. The ascending mind of humanity is to meet the descending truth of divine revelation.
> >
> > 2. Jesus exerts his authority by making us free. Slavery to Christ is glorious and strange.
> >
> > 3. Having subjected us to Himself, Jesus makes us the medium of His authority to the world.[9]

---

9. E.Y. Mullins, "The Lordship of Christ," *Baptist and Reflector* (August 24, 1911), 3-4.

Mullins could also preach with great unction and eloquence as this excerpt from a sermon on the cross indicates. Mullins's words built a visual imagery.

> But the saving significance of the cross relates in part to the effect on Satan. Christ came to cast out the prince of this world. Marvelous is the method employed to accomplish it. He does it not with thunderbolts of wrath, not with fiery chariots and an army of angelic cohorts. He conquers Satan by surrendering to his power. "Come," says Jesus to the arch enemy, "bind these hands and these feet with your strongest chain, transfix me with your most deadly arrow, death; close these eyes, blanch these lips, still this throbbing heart, entomb me in rock and seal it and guard it well." And the sepulchre smacks its satisfied lips over the cold clay of the dead Christ. Laugh demons! Exult Satan! Weep angels! Gather in little groups, ye broken-hearted disciples, and pour out your grief to one another. But hark! That was the rumbling of an earthquake. Look! That flash of light before the dawn is an angel dropping through space to the door of the tomb, and behold, within the sepulchre the blush of life mantles the face of the sleeper; he sits up and calmly disrobes himself of the grave-clothes and steps forth the victor over death forevermore. Satan has no other weapon of attack. He has done his worst and failed. He is conquered. The pent-up tides of life which have been surging in the bosom of Jesus have at last broken through their bounds, and the wilderness and the solitary place can rejoice and the desert can blossom as the rose, and all the choirs of creation can catch up the song of redemption and pour forth their floods of praise to God who loveth and redeemeth the world.[10]

Mullins maintained close touch with everyday life, as is evident in the various homely analogies and metaphors found in his sermons. For example, "You cannot hatch goslings from doorknobs"; "going through college does not make a scholar any more than going through a garage makes a man an automobile"; "joining a church does not make one a Christian any more than looking through a telescope makes one an astronomer."[11]

---

10. E.Y. Mullins, "A Kingdom Built on a Cross," *The Southern Baptist Pulpit*, ed. J.F. Love (Philadelphia: American Baptist Publication Society, 1895), 249-50.

11. Henry Tiffany, "The Services and Servants of the Seminary," *Review and Expositor*, 48 (April 1951), 199.

Profound thinking expressed in simple language and pictured in everyday life made E.Y. Mullins one of Southern Baptists' finest preachers.

James Bruton Gambrell (1841-1921)

If James Bruton (J.B.) Gambrell had not been called of God to special ministry, he might have been noted as one of America's great adventurers. He scouted federal field positions in northern Virginia for the Confederate army during the Civil War. Frequently, federal troops pursued him on his return to Confederate territory. Often, he hid in the barn of a southern sympathizer. During those hide-outs, he became acquainted with his friends' daughter. One night, on his way back to Confederate headquarters, he married her. Gambrell literally fulfilled his scouting mission by midnight, was married at 1 a.m. to Mary T. Corbell of Nansemond County, Virginia, and reported to headquarters eight hours later. Although the rest of Gambrell's life was tame by comparison to his Civil War service and his daring wedding behind federal lines, the same sense of determination and singleness of purpose characterized his ministerial life.

Gambrell was born August 21, 1841, in Anderson County, South Carolina. In 1842, the Gambrells moved to Mississippi. He received advanced education at the University of Mississippi and became the first editor of *The Baptist Record,* Mississippi's Baptist state newspaper in 1877. Beginning in 1893, he served a three-year term as president of Mercer University. From 1896 until 1921 Gambrell served in Texas as superintendent of missions, editor of the *Baptist Standard,* briefly as a faculty member at Southwestern Seminary, and as executive secretary of the Consolidated Board of the Baptist General Convention of Texas.

> E.C. Routh described Gambrell as a champion of "the plain people." The plain people understood his message. He was their voice. He loved them and served them. Few men in any generation were as quick to discern the needs of humanity and as competent to express such needs as he.[12]

---

12. E.C. Routh, *Life Story of Dr. J.B. Gambrell* (Oklahoma City: published by the author, 1929), 175.

Routh described Gambrell as a steadfast man whose life was characterized by simplicity.

Gambrell's sermons were almost always topical. Many of his published sermons do not indicate any text and the biblical authority for his sermons was casual, and occasionally secondary. The subject of most of his sermons related to some contemporary issue. Gambrell was not a strong expositor, but was strong in integrating various Scriptures with the subject of the sermon. He was especially adept in the use of appealing illustrations, and in the use of direct application.

An innovative and popular sermon of Gambrell's was titled, "Up Fool Hill." The sermon had no listed text and was preached as a story.

> Fool Hill lies just where the undulating lowlands of boyhood rise sharply up to the highlands of manhood. It is climbed only by big boys. Just which way he will go is an unknown thing.
>
> When you notice the boy feeling of his upper lip, (and a little reddening of the skin), look sharp. The boy will soon begin to climb. The problem is to get him up the hill and in good repair. That done, you have blessed the world with a man.
>
> Our boy is among us. He is an unturned cake. He is worth cooking. Two worlds are interested in that young fool, and underneath his folly there lies sleeping maybe a great preacher, teacher or other dignitary.[13]

"Three Steps Up," a sermon he preached in 1895 at the Jubilee Session of the Southern Baptist Convention, shows a deeper, more reflective Gambrell. The sermon was developed with three divisions. The biblical authority was direct, and there was a balance of explanation, application, and illustration. The conclusion departed from the points of the sermon. We can only deduce that Gambrell made indirect application of the text in the conclusion, both to himself and to the congregation.

> Text: Philippians 1:9-11
>
> This letter to the Philippians is a beautiful love letter. Yet, as good as this church was, it was capable of being better. The apos-

13. J.B. Gambrell, *Ten Years in Texas* (Dallas: Baptist Standard, 1909), 29-33.

tle wanted them to go up higher. The foundation for this step up was laid in his prayer for them.

I. The first part of this prayer is that love might abound more and more.

II. This love is to be in knowledge.

III. This love is to be in knowledge, tempered by judgment.

Brethren, the thought in my mind now is, that I shall fill all the remaining days of my life with the fruits of righteousness.[14]

Carter Helm Jones (1861-1946)

Carter Helm Jones was a popular preacher, especially in the first three decades of the twentieth century. Born in Nelson County, Virginia, November 30, 1861, his father was a Baptist pastor. Jones graduated from Richmond College in 1882, and Southern Seminary in 1885. In 1890, he became pastor of First Baptist Church, Knoxville, Tennessee, and in 1891 preached the annual sermon to the Southern Baptist Convention. In 1894, Jones became pastor of the McFerran Memorial Baptist Church in Louisville, Kentucky. Three years later he accepted the call of a sister church in the same city, Broadway Baptist, which soon became the most overcrowded church in Louisville. Jones also pastored the First Baptist churches of Lynchburg, Virginia; Oklahoma City, Oklahoma; Seattle, Washington; Philadelphia, Pennsylvania; and Murfreesboro, Tennessee.

Jones became involved in the Whitsitt controversy while in Louisville, and continued to defend Dr. Whitsitt long after Whitsitt had resigned as president of Southern Baptist Theological Seminary. Several Baptist state papers reported Jones's lament on Whitsitt's forced resignation: "Thus it has been from Christ to Galileo, from Socrates to Whitsitt, the last victim of combined ignorance and malice."

Jones exemplified oratorical skills in his sermon content but utilized a conversational style in his delivery. In his welcoming speech to the messengers of the Southern Baptist Convention,

---

14. J.B. Gambrell, "Three Steps Up," *The Southern Baptist Pulpit,* ed. by J.F. Love, (Philadelphia: American Baptist Publication Society, 1895), 180-190.

meeting in Oklahoma City in 1912, Jones regaled the congregation:

> This is an impressive moment. I have stood on the top of Cheops and looked down through the valley of the Nile through forty centuries of mysteries. I have stood on the mountains overlooking Jerusalem and dreamed and thought and sobbed and loved. I have stood on the Acropolis with that poem in stone behind me, the Parthenon, that has baffled all modern art. I have walked where Plato talked with Socrates, where Aristotle taught and where Demosthenes thundered. I have stood in Roman Forum girt about with ruins. This is a greater moment than that. That was yesterday, yesterday of mystery of religion, culture, power. Today I see the evangels of the kingdom, prophets of tomorrow. Come in messengers of the Lord.[15]

Most of Jones's sermons relied on a text of one or two verses and were developed topically. A few sermons were textual. None of Jones's sermons available to us is expository. Almost all of the sermons had secondary biblical authority. His introductions varied in length and in approach. On one occasion, the introduction was simply the reading of the text. On other occasions, the introductions were several paragraphs long, using either an extended illustration or the historical background of the text. Jones preferred rhetorical outlines, but used a homily on a few occasions. The conclusions always contained a direct appeal.

One of the textual sermons by Jones was unusually captivating.

> Text: Deuteronomy 32:11-12
>
> Title: The Eagle
>
> Introduction: This is a bit of Moses' Song which he sang to Israel in the golden gloaming of his wonderful life. God treated Israel as a mother eagle treats the little ones in her nest.
>
> Body:
> I. The nesting time ("As an eagle stirreth up her nest").
> The nesting time is a time of feeding and sweet fellowship and all is happiness.

---

15. "Carter Helm Jones," *The Christian Index* (June 13, 1912), 1.

   II. The testing time ("taketh them, beareth them on her wings").

     The eaglets will never be eagles if they never leave the nest. They must try their wings.

   III. The hovering help ("so the Lord alone did lead him").

     God breaks the nest to stir us out of our complacency.

     Conclusion: I give you God's eaglehood and pray that we too may soar. Some sweet day, as we fly higher . . . the everlasting gates shall be lifted. . . .[16]

"The Temple in the Heart" is an example of one of Jones's topical sermons.

     Text: 2 Chronicles 6:8-9

     Introduction: One of David's laments was, "I dwell in a house of cedar, but the ark of God dwells within curtains."

   I. The temple in the heart. In these hearts, these brains, these inner natures of ours, we carry our dreams, we carry our loves, we carry our purposes, we carry our plans, we carry our ideals.

   II. The temples that never leave the heart. The unfulfilled ideals. The songs that are unsung, and yet they are music. Procrastination, perhaps a lack of fixed industry cause the tragedy of a temple that never leaves the heart.

   III. The temples that can never leave the heart. Temples like David's. Sometimes there are divine limits on temples we want to build.

   IV. The glory of these heart temples. No noble thought, no great purpose, no aspiring endeavor ever dwelt in the soul . . . that did not leave a fragrance, a chastened beauty.

     Conclusion: We must do our best even if we must leave the other man to finish it.[17]

William WARREN LANdRUM (1853-1926)

William Warren (W.W.) Landrum, along with Carter Jones, built a bridge for Southern Baptist preaching from a purely pedantic, oratorical style to the beginnings of what would later be known as an oratorical-conversational style of preaching. Landrum did this by the simple device of transliterating scriptural events into a present tense narrative. For example:

16. Carter H. Jones, "The Eagle," *Prophetic Patriotism* (Nashville: Broadman Press, 1941), 67-78.

17. Ibid., 55-66.

> Thomas hears all this, but doubts everything. He is slow to believe Jesus will raise Lazarus from the dead. On the contrary, he believes the Jews will kill Jesus the moment he sets foot on the soil of Judea. He actually sees no hope of escape for his Lord.[18]

This use of the historical present tense is common now, but it was unique then. Congregations found this "fresh" approach interesting.

Landrum was born in Macon, Georgia, in 1853. His father, a Baptist pastor, baptized him in 1867. Landrum graduated from Brown University in 1872 and from Southern Seminary in 1874. His pastorates included First Baptist Church, Shreveport, Louisiana; First Baptist, Augusta, Georgia; Second Baptist, Richmond, Virginia; First Baptist, Atlanta, Georgia; Broadway Baptist, Louisville, Kentucky; and First Baptist, Russellville, Kentucky. He also taught at Bethel College in Kentucky from 1919 to 1926.

Landrum was twice elected vice president of the Southern Baptist Convention, and served as a trustee of many denominational agencies. He actively supported the development of the Cooperative Program.

Landrum preferred to preach from one or two verse texts. The use of present tense for scriptural events kept him keyed in on direct biblical authority in most of the sermons. He preferred to use an outline for his sermons and his outlines complemented the titles of his sermons, which were unusually terse. One sermon was titled simply "All." Landrum used a balance of explanation, application, and illustration. Argumentation does not appear in his sermons, possibly because he detested controversy.

To sample Landrum's preaching, a synopsis of the sermon "All" is offered.

Text: Matthew 28:19-20

Introduction: Brief discussion of Jesus and the apostles.

I. "All authority" is our first mountain. Jesus Christ has all authority.

---

18. W.W. Landrum, *Settled in the Sanctuary* (Nashville: Sunday School Board of the Southern Baptist Convention, 1925), 135.

II. All authority ordered that his message be preached to "All nations."

III. This all authority issues to all nations "All commands."

IV. The all authority is with us "All ways," or, literally, he is with us "all days."

Landrum especially liked to introduce his sermons by surveying the persons in the text. His finest moment with this kind of introduction (even though he reverted to past tense) came in the sermon, "Gambling at Golgotha":

> Look at the Roman guard. We do no violence to the text if we put it this way: Christ they crucified and then gambled for his garments. Look at the Roman guard, I say. Who so near the expiring Christ as they? Why, they could actually place their hands on "the Lamb of God which taketh away the sin of the world." They were nearer than the weeping women in the distance, nearer than John the beloved disciple, nearer than Mary the agonized mother. They had leisure for reflection, for we read, "And sitting down they watched him there." Hours of meditation on the meaning of the Lord's death offered them exceptional opportunities for learning its relation to their eternal welfare.
>
> The centurion, their captain, was impressed. He confessed the Christ to be "a good man" and "a Son of God." How did the soldiers improve the time? They went to gambling. At the supreme tragedy of human history they went to gambling. Oh, wonder of wonders, they fell agambling. From the Christ of God, the Savior of the world, the Lord of all things, these rude, rough Roman regulars received only the paltry, pitiful rags which covered Christ's body. Instead of everlasting life they received only Jesus' cast-off clothes. And they gambled about them. And from that day to this the glassy eye of the avaricious gambler has looked on the Savior's death as an insignificant occurrence beneath notice.

Landrum's gift for finding human-interest qualities in the Bible and sharing them in his sermons was a first step for Southern Baptists. Beginning with Landrum, Southern Baptist preaching moved from a formal oratorical style to a more appealing conversational style. In a sense, Southern Baptist preaching has never entirely left its oratorical roots. W.W. Landrum, however, grafted new branches onto what was become an old tree.

GEORGE WHITE McDANIEL (1875-1927)

George W. McDaniel was born in Grimes County, Texas, November 30, 1875. George gave his life to Jesus and joined First Baptist Church, Navasota, Texas. A few years later, he enrolled at Baylor University. After graduation at Baylor, he immediately enrolled at Southern Seminary and received a degree in 1900. McDaniel pastored First Baptist Church, Temple, Texas, and the Gaston Avenue Baptist Church in Dallas before accepting the call to pastor the First Baptist Church of Richmond, Virginia. He served twenty-three years at the old and prestigious Richmond church.

Most of McDaniel's sermons had secondary biblical authority. His sermons were notable for clarity, singleness of purpose, and for their immediate and direct application to his congregations. His explanation of the text was not expansive, but there was always enough to set the foundation for illustrative material and for the application he chose to make. Most of McDaniel's published sermons were based on a one-verse text. His style was more conversational than oratorical.

McDaniel's inaugural sermon in Richmond typified his preaching style.

> Text: Acts 11:29
>
> Title: To What Intent?
>
> Introduction: To what intent have you called me to be your pasto
>
> I. You have not called me to look at the temporalities of the church. That is for the deacons.
>
> II. You have not called me to wear another man's armor, nor to wear an armor which you may make. Just as David could not wear Saul's armor, so the pastor must find his own way.
>
> III. You have not sent me to help the "Old First" hold her own. You must grow or decay.
>
> Conclusion: (Goals for First Baptist Richmond to achieve in the next several years.)[19]

19. George W. McDaniel, "To What Intent," *Religious Herald* (February 2, 1905), 2.

McDaniel preached the annual sermon at the Southern Baptist Convention in 1905. It is a creative sermon with a pertinent message for that convention and ranks as an outstanding example of relating the Bible to a contemporary congregation.

Text: Exodus 13:30-31; Deuteronomy 1:26

Title: Southern Baptists at Kadesh-Barnea

Introduction: The Israelites entered Egypt a family and emerged a nation. The experience of Israel in Egypt is paralleled by Baptists in the South. Baptists have multiplied in this sunny Southland faster than the Israelites multiplied in Egypt.

Body: The position of Israel at the border of the Promised Land is analogous to that which we occupy today. They refused to go up. No class of people is larger than its faith. It is not the number of our members, nor the mass of our future that brings victory. It is that "Jehovah is among us."

There are supreme hours which come to denominations. I dare to say we live in such an hour. When I reflect that 11,000 churches in the bounds of this denomination gave nothing to save the heathen, I feel like putting on sackcloth and ashes. My brethren we dare not stop where we are.

Only as the Baptist denomination serves God by enriching the lives of men will it be justified at the bar of public opinion.

Conclusion: This is our day of opportunity and responsibility. We must write the articles of our faith in the imperative rather than the subjunctive mood. Here, if anywhere, and now, if ever, Baptists must come into their inheritance. Shall people fail or fatten? Nay, the fires of missionary zeal burn away the dross.[20]

MoNROE ElMON Dodd (1878-1952)

Dodd preached his first sermon on April 8, 1900. His text was 1 Corinthians 2:2: "For I determined not to know anything among you, save Jesus Christ, and him crucified." Dodd declared to himself that Scripture would be his text for the rest of his life. His preaching spanned fifty-two years.

20. George W. McDaniel, "Southern Baptists at Kadesh-Barnea," *Baptist Standard* (May 28, 1914), 6-7, and (June 4, 1914), 11-12.

Monroe Elmon (M.E.) Dodd was born in Brazil, Tennessee, September 8, 1878. He received a B.A. from Union University in Jackson, Tennessee, in 1904 and was ordained to the ministry while a student. He never attended seminary, but he was known as a scholarly lecturer on the New Testament. Dodd attended the Chatauqua Bible Study circuit regularly; these conferences, some of which were led by G. Campbell Morgan, had a strong impact on his sermon style. In a letter to one of the Chatauqua conference leaders, he testified that his first inspiration for expository preaching resulted from attending those Bible conferences.

In 1904, about the time he entered his first full-time pastorate at Fulton, Kentucky, he married Emma Savage, whose father was president of Union University. Dodd had struggled with a call to foreign missions early in his ministry. The next year, he and his wife left Fulton as missionaries. Their five-month stint as missionaries was shadowed by hardships, including a train wreck enroute to the field. News of their difficulties reached Fulton, and the congregation urged the Dodds to return. By this time, the Dodds were certain they had misinterpreted God's will and returned to their pastorate. Dodd maintained an interest in mission work and in 1934, as president of the Southern Baptist Convention, made several tours of mission fields.

Dodd's administrative abilities were exercised not only in his pastorate but also in various denominational activities. He served as president of the Louisiana Convention in 1927 and 1928[21] and as Southern Baptist Convention president in 1934.[22] His most significant contribution to the denomination was his service on committees. He was on the committee that recommended establishing the Baptist Bible Institute in New Orleans (later New Orleans Baptist Theological Seminary) in 1924. The next year, he brought a special committee's findings to the Convention and recommended the acceptance of the Cooperative Program. The idea for the program was the result of the committee's survey of denominational leaders.[23]

---

21. Ramay, 378.
22. *Annual*, Southern Baptist Convention, (1934), 54.
23. Austin Tucker, "Monroe Elmon Dodd and His Preaching" (Th.D. dissertation, Southwestern Baptist Theological Seminary, 1971), 26.

Service on the Convention's radio committee led to a pioneer broadcast ministry. First Baptist Church, Shreveport, built its own radio station in 1922 and was assigned the call letters KDKX. The radio ministry was expanded in 1929 to KWKH, a Shreveport CBS Network affiliate station with fifty thousand watts. Dodd estimated his listening audience in 1930 at two to four million persons.[24] In 1934, the Federal Communications Commission reassigned the clear channel frequency to WWL in New Orleans and KWKH reverted to a regional station with much less kilowatt power. The preaching program continued until 1944 when CBS announced it would fill the Sunday evening time with a another program.

In 1940, Dodd began work with the Southern Baptist Radio Committee. Due in part to his experience in broadcasting, the committee asked him to be the first speaker on the new program, "The Baptist Hour." The program, which continues to be one of the most popular of the programs produced by the Southern Baptist Radio and Television Commission, was launched on January 5, 1941.

Dodd varied his approaches to preaching. Many of his sermons were expository. The biblical authority in his sermons ranges from direct to casual. In addition to his published sermons, Dodd's sermon notes and correspondence are on file in the archival section at Southwestern's Roberts Library. His sermons reflect variety not only in approach but also in length of biblical texts, which ranged from no announced text to multiple-passage texts. Most of the sermons are balanced in their use of explanation, application, and illustration.

As an example of Dodd's preaching, consider his expository sermon, "His Bodily Resurrection."

> Text: 1 Corinthians 15:1-26
>
> Introduction: The tombs of great men are still occupied—Washington in Mt. Vernon, Grant in New York City, Lincoln in Springfield.

---

24. M.E. Dodd, "The Radio and Religion," typed address in Dodd Collection of materials in the archival section of Roberts Library, Southwestern Baptist Theological Seminary, Ft. Worth, Texas, 1934, 2-3.

Visiting the tomb of Jesus is a markedly different experience.

I. A fact stated (1 Corinthians 15:1-4). Paul does not set forth an argument here; he simply states a fact.

We need not burden ourselves with argument. The plain fact is He is risen.

II. A fact proven (1 Corinthians 15:5-11). The evidence is presented by unimpeachable witnesses. In fact, it requires more faith to believe some of the theories which seek to explain away the resurrection of Christ than it does to believe in the fact itself.

III. A fact essential (1 Corinthians 15:12-19). He died for our redemption and arose for our justification. Pagans and heathen have had hope in great teachers, but there is one hope they never had, for the resurrection of the dead is a definitely Christian doctrine.

IV. A triumphant fact (1 Corinthians 15:20-26). Jesus came to destroy every enemy of man: sorrow, sickness, sin, and death.

Conclusion: We rejoice that death has been conquered by Him.[25]

Other Preachers

Fernando Coello McConnell

Fernando Coello McConnell had a powerful voice and a forceful delivery. Consequently, contemporary preachers re-named him Forensic Cyclonic McConnell. McConnell's daughter wrote:

> I was (five years old) when I was first influenced by the power and quality of (my father's) voice. In the tone of his voice, Father imparted to me a realization of God which never left me.[26]

McConnell was born in Clay County, North Carolina, August 2, 1856. He was ordained in 1880, graduated from Mercer University, and enrolled for some courses at Southern Seminary. His longest pastorate was at Druid Hills Baptist Church in Atlanta, Georgia, from 1915 until his death January 12, 1929.

25. M.E. Dodd, "His Bodily Resurrection," *The Christ Whom We Worship* (Shreveport: Journal Publishing Co., 1930), 71-95.
26. Christine McConnell Rousseau, *The Turquoise Path* (Nashville: Broadman Press, 1943), 75-76.

A few of McConnell's sermons were printed in Baptist periodicals. He was known as a powerful evangelistic and as an effective doctrinal preacher. The sermon "The Angels as Students of Christ's Love to Men," preached November 9, 1902, at the Convention of Texas Baptists serves as an example of his approach to preaching. The introduction was extraordinarily long, comprising thirty percent of the sermon. McConnell used four points to develop the body of the sermon.

    I. The first lesson is one of wondrous love.

    II. The other thing is our inheritance in heaven.

    III. The angels also wonder of our transformation (through grace).

    IV. The angels are students of the sufferings of Christ and the glory that shall follow.[27]

Edwin Charles Dargan

Edwin Charles Dargan made a monumental contribution to homiletical studies with his *A History of Preaching*.[28] He was born in Darlington, South Carolina, November 17, 1852. He graduated from Furman University in 1873 and Southern Baptist Theological Seminary in 1877. He became professor of homiletics at Southern in 1892, and returned to the pastorate in 1907, serving the First Baptist Church of Macon, Georgia, for ten years. He accepted the position of editorial secretary of the Southern Baptist Sunday School Board until his retirement in 1927.

Most of Dargan's sermons had secondary biblical authority. His preaching tended to be didactic and overbalanced in the use of explanation. One of his students once testified that Dargan taught that sermons should be written like telegrams with all superfluous words omitted. "The Parable of the Lost and Found" is an example.

> Text: Luke 15:1-3
>
> We have here not three parables, but one. Losing and finding furnish the theme, and finding is the chief point of emphasis.

27. F.C. McConnell, "The Angels as Students of Christ's Love to Men," *Baptist Standard* (December 4, 1902), 6-8.

28. E.C. Dargan, *A History of Preaching*, Vol. I (New York: A.C. Armstrong & Son, 1906); Vol. II (New York: George H. Doran & Co., 1912).

I. The sheep lost and found. The picture presented is very simple and clear.

II. A coin lost and found. In the first section it was a man and his sheep. Outdoor economy. In this section, it is a woman and her coin. Indoor economy.

III. A lost and found son. The parable is a climax and now we come to its height.

Let us repeat, with emphasis, that the key-note of the parable is the joy of finding that which was lost.[29]

John Richard Sampey

John Richard Sampey delighted in preaching sermons on Old Testament persons. This is not surprising since Sampey was a biblical scholar who taught Old Testament and Hebrew and served as president of Southern Seminary for many years.

Born at Fort Deposit, Alabama, September 27, 1863, he graduated from Howard College and Southern Seminary. His teaching career at Southern began in 1885, the year that he graduated. His term as president of Southern began in 1928, shortly after the death of E.Y. Mullins. Sampey served as pastor of several small churches in Kentucky. His students affectionately called him "Tiglath-Pileser" or "Old Tig."

Sampey's sermons were published in several Baptist periodicals and in *Ten Vital Messages,*[30] a collection of messages preached on WHHS in Louisville in 1944-45. Unfortunately, none of these messages were on Old Testament characters. Most of the sermons had direct biblical authority. Sampey seemed as comfortable with a homily as he did with rhetorical outlines. Explanation, application, and illustration are equally balanced and the conclusions contain direct appeal, combined occasionally with a summary of the sermon. Sampey preferred to use only a brief text, but did provide a contextual study in the sermon.

The sermons included in *Ten Vital Messages* are all practical, and expressed in simple language. "Faith Overcoming Doubt," preached May 13, 1945, is an example.

---

29. E.C. Dargan, *The Changeless Christ* (Chicago: Fleming H. Revell Co., 1918), 104-120.

30. John R. Sampey, *Ten Vital Messages* (Nashville: Broadman Press, 1946).

Text: Mark 9:24

Introduction: The words of our text were spoken by a father in deep distress. The nine disciples could not cast out the evil spirit because of a lack of prayer and the lack of faith which comes through prayer. After the night on the mountain, Jesus was full of power to heal.

Body:

I. There is an affirmation of faith, "I believe." The father had been tossed between faith and doubt; but as he looked into the face of Jesus, faith revived.

II. A prayer for the removal of doubt, "Help mine unbelief." One of the common causes of unbelief is the failure of Christ's disciples to measure up to His standards. There is no better way to overcome doubt than to spend time daily in communion with the Heavenly Father.

Conclusion: We need faith in a God of righteous love.[31]

Edwin McNeal Poteat, Sr.

Edwin McNeal Poteat, Sr. had a checkered career as pastor, educator, and administrator of various offices, in and out of Southern Baptist churches and schools. He was a member of the Northern Baptist Convention at times, and for five years he taught at Shanghai Baptist College in China.

Poteat was born in Caswell County, North Carolina, February 6, 1861. He was serving as a professor at Furman University when he died June 25, 1937.

A powerful expository preacher, Potent's sermons were clearly organized, conversational in style, and had direct biblical authority. Besides explanation, Poteat's sermons contained a rich variety of illustrative material, and indirect application. Some of Poteat's sermons were published in *The Withered Fig Tree* and *The Religion of the Lord's Prayer*, but the most representative of his sermons was preached in chapel at Furman University, September 27, 1903.

Text: Philippians 3:10

Title: That I May Know Him

Introduction: This text introduces us to the knowledge of Christ as the highest pursuit of the human mind.

---

31. Ibid., 11-19.

I. Knowledge of Christ is the highest knowledge.
   1. It is the highest knowledge because it is of the Highest Person. To know the world is preliminary to a higher knowledge of Christ.
   2. The knowledge of Christ is highest because it is eternal life.
   3. The knowledge of Christ is highest because it binds all other knowledge together.
II. Seek the knowledge of Christ enthusiastically.
III. How shall we set about knowing Him?
   1. Through critical investigation.
   2. Through faith.
   3. Through fellowship in suffering.[32]

Lee Rutland Scarborough

Lee Rutland Scarborough became the first professor of evangelism in the United States in 1908, the inaugural year of Southwestern Baptist Seminary. B.H. Carroll witnessed and appreciated Scarborough's passion for evangelism and believed that he would be an ideal professor.

Born in Colfax, Louisiana, July 4, 1870, the Scarboroughs moved to Texas in 1874, where Lee later learned to love and live the cowboy life. Scarborough graduated from Baylor and Yale. He pastored the First Baptist churches of Cameron and Abilene, Texas, before joining the faculty of Southwestern Baptist Theological Seminary in 1908. In 1914, shortly after Carroll's death, Scarborough became president of the seminary. Carroll's last words to Scarborough were, "Keep the school lashed to the cross!" Scarborough served as president until 1942.

All of Scarborough's published sermons have an evangelistic objective and most of them are developed topically. Biblical authority was either direct or secondary. Although his sermons were not expository, Scarborough used brief explanations as exposition of the text throughout the sermon. Application and illustration were used heavily. The sermons were each developed as a homily with strong transition sentences to assist the listeners. The conclusions depended heavily on direct appeal.

32. E.M. Poteat, "The Highest Knowledge," *The Baptist Courier* (October 15, 1903), 6-7.

Typical of Scarborough's sermons is one titled, "Hell," for which no text is listed.

> Introduction: Two hundred and thirty-four times, nearly one verse for every chapter in the New Testament, God says that there is a place of eternal punishment. If life's road twenty-six miles long had on it two hundred and thirty-four sign boards saying, "This road leads to hell," I think I would go another road.

> (Fourteen Scripture passages quoted all relating to eternal perdition.)

> Body: Luke 16:19-31 is a message from a man in hell. God doesn't say it is a parable. Since you have to meet the truth of God up yonder, you might as well get used to it down here.

> This man had eyes, voice, and memory in hell. In fact you will remember this sermon if you go to hell. Think of it! In hell forever and memory fresh!

> Conclusion: God help you tonight to see that there is a hell, and the reason you are going is you won't give up your sins. Tonight, trust the Lord Jesus as your Savior.[33]

Jefferson Davis Ray

Jefferson Davis Ray was born in Mission Valley, Texas, November 20, 1860. Remembered as a professor of homiletics at Southwestern Seminary from 1907 to 1944, he pastored several churches before beginning his teaching career. In 1879, he attended the National School of Elocution and Oratory in Philadelphia which, no doubt, contributed to his effectiveness in the classroom, and to his effectiveness in the oral interpretation of Scripture. In a eulogy, one writer claimed:

> Just to hear him read the story of the prodigal son was better than most sermons we have ever heard on the story. To him there was no excuse nor justification for failure . . . of the preacher in reading the Scriptures . . . in such a way as to enable the people to get the full picture and meaning of the inspired Word.[34]

---

33. L.R. Scarborough, "Hell," *Prepare to Meet God* (New York: George H. Doran Co., 1922), 42-59.

34. David M. Gardner, "Dr. Ray Passes Away," *Southwestern News* (September, 1951), 2.

Most of his sermons were expository, using direct biblical authority. His sermons, like the man, were plainspoken and emphatic.

> Text: Matthew 3:1
>
> Title: The Preaching of John the Baptist
>
> Preaching has ever been God's chief agency for the spread of the gospel.
>
> I. Consider the manner of John's preaching. There was a blend of sweet humility and dogmatic boldness. It was artlessly direct and personal.
>
> II. Consider the matter of John's preaching. These three words— sin, salvation and service—are the sum of the matter of John's preaching.
>
> III. Consider the results of John's preaching. The people heard him, were stirred by him, and it cost him his life.
>
> The voice of John is not dead. Immortal thus is the voice of every true, God-sent messenger.[35]

ARchibAld ThomAs RobERTSON

Archibald Thomas Robertson, born in Pittsylvania County, Virginia, November 6, 1863, was to New Testament and Greek studies what his father-in-law, John A. Broadus, was to homiletical studies. From 1888 until his death in 1934, Robertson was a professor of New Testament Interpretation at Southern Seminary.

Robertson became an outstanding expository preacher as his knowledge of biblical languages grew. His sermons had direct biblical authority and were simple. Robertson tended to be didactic, but this was cleverly balanced by his dry humor and by the use of appealing, human-interest illustrative material. These qualities are evident in his sermon "The Living Sacrifice."

> Text: Romans 12:1
>
> There is prejudice today against the word sacrifice, but Paul uses it here in the metaphorical sense for consecration to the service of God.
>
> I. Paul's appeal to life. The first eleven chapters gave a wonderful discussion of the great doctrine of the God-kind of righteous-

---

35. Jeff D. Ray, "The Preaching of John the Baptist," *The Baptist Standard* (March 23, 1905), 6.

ness. Now, Paul turns to practical exhortations. Paul's "there-fores" are always impressive and not merely mechanical expletives, as is sometimes the case with preachers.

II. The ground of the appeal. We can trust God's knowledge, power, and love when we cannot see.

III. The whole self at the service of God. The bodies are to be presented to God, not just the spirits. There are plenty of so-called Christians today who let the devil have their bodies and seek to serve God with their spirits. The devil in the end will get both. A man once willed his soul to the devil. The devil already had it.

IV. Non-conformity with the world. It is the present tense of habitual action that is here prohibited.

V. Transformation of the life. It is the present tense again and means "a perpetual progression."

VI. Disclosing God's will by the life. The highest test of any life is doing the will of God.

"God willing" should be our attitude always.[36]

James Marion Frost

James Marion Frost once wrote: "My sermons cost me much work—though I fear others may not think so."[37] Frost is remembered as founder of the Baptist Sunday School Board. He also had a distinguished career as a pastor in five churches before assuming full-time responsibilities at the Sunday School Board in 1896.

For all his belief in literature as a means to teach the Bible and to spread Baptist belief, Frost could not write his sermons: "In preparation the pen is . . . a hindrance. I go to the pulpit without writing a word . . . not even an outline."[38]

An 1896 sermon commemorating B.H. Carroll's twenty-fifth anniversary as a pastor was published in the *Baptist Standard*.

36. A.T. Robertson, "The Living Sacrifice," *Jesus as a Soul Winner* (New York: Fleming H. Revell Co., 1937), 65-73. (Also see Robertson, *Passing the Torch* [New York: Revell Co., 1934].)

37. J.M. Frost, "How I Prepare My Sermons," *Baptist and Reflector* (February 7, 1895), 3.

38. Ibid.

Text: 2 Corinthians 1:14; 1 Thessalonians 2:19-20

Title: The Pastor's Joy and Crown of Rejoicing

The pastor's joy and crown of rejoicing are found in his people.

I. His joy in serving his people.

II. His joy in the help his people give him.

III. His joy in the achievements wrought out under his leadership.

IV. His joy and theirs as they shall stand together in the final consummation of things.

W.W. MELTON

W.W. Melton was born January 19, 1879, on a farm in Texas. Early educational opportunities were so limited that he enrolled in a junior college when he was twenty-two years old, and spent six years preparing to attend Baylor University. Melton graduated from Baylor and Southwestern Seminary, and he served as pastor of the Seventh and James Baptist Church in Waco (adjacent to the Baylor campus) for forty-one years. He was executive secretary of the Baptist General Convention of Texas for four-and-a-half years.

Melton's sermons were richly expositional, although they were presented in a conversational style. Most of his sermons contained either direct or secondary biblical authority and the application was strong and direct. Melton did not use many illustrations, but most of those he did use were taken from the Bible. Many of his sermons were built on rhetorical outlines, but some of his best sermons were formal homilies.

A typical sermon of Melton's was titled "Was Jesus Divine?"

Text: Matthew 3:17

Introduction: The Christian religion rests upon four fundamental facts: the deity of Jesus, the vicarious suffering of Jesus, the bodily resurrection of Jesus, and the literal return of Jesus to earth.

Some try to defend these doctrines, as if their security depended on human help. God does not need defense, nor does the Bible, nor do these great fundamental facts.

Body: The structure of the Bible makes an interesting portrayal of a divine plot. The fifty-third chapter of Isaiah gives us the most vivid picture of Christ. Jesus was the full expression of the

Father's will, love, and plan. In Him God had clothed Himself with humanity.

Many times did the Father acknowledge Him as Son. In the gospel of John there are more than one hundred references to the relationship of Christ to his Father. We have no full revelation of God, save Jesus.

Conclusion: He is the starting point. There is no meaning to such words as faith, righteousness, service, heaven, peace, or eternal life without Christ, the Son of God.[39]

John Franklyn Norris

John Franklyn Norris was born September 18, 1877, in Dadeville, Alabama. The Norris family moved to Hubbard City (now Hubbard), Texas, in 1888. Norris knew abject poverty. As a boy, when he was fifteen years old, he was shot in the abdomen by a man arguing with his father. Norris's mother had tremendous influence over him, especially as he lay close to death from his wound. During his arduous recovery, Norris began to visualize his life as one talking to large crowds of people about God.

Norris had made a profession of faith in Jesus in 1890, but he was not baptized until 1895. Catlett Smith, pastor of the Hubbard City Baptist Church, taught Norris how to communicate the Word of God. Smith was full of violent emotionalism and mannerisms, which appealed to Norris.

Norris graduated from Baylor and Southern Seminary. B.H. Carroll, in 1909, recommended Norris as pastor of the First Baptist Church of Fort Worth. In 1907, he bought controlling interest in the *Baptist Standard*. Controversy filled his career. Norris's volatile personality had its impact on Southern Baptist life. He accused Baptist colleges of teaching evolution while ignoring the Genesis account of creation. He charged that Southern Baptist seminaries were full of liberalism and he opposed the Seventy-Five Million campaign. He resented Southern Baptists' resistance to some of his premillennial views and he was excluded from participation in Southern Baptist life.

39. W.W. Melton, "Was Jesus Divine?" *The Christian Heritage* (New York City: The American Press, 1959), 5-10.

Norris's published sermons were mostly topical with secondary and casual biblical authority. His sermons were published from a stenographer's notes. The possibility exists, therefore, that these sermons may not be accurately reported. As published, however, the sermons tend to ramble across the spectrum of religious thought. Frequently, it is difficult to see how consecutive paragraphs relate to one another, the text, or to the title. Norris had great passion for the cause of Christ, and he defended what he believed to be correct interpretation of the Bible. His sermons lacked clarity, and, more importantly, a strong exposition of the text. Norris used little explanation but a great deal of application and illustration. The paragraphs were often terse and not well developed.

He was fond of using long lists of reasons or rules to verify the thesis or topic of his sermons. For instance, in a sermon on Romans 8:28, Norris moved from the introduction to the body by saying, "There are fourteen divine reasons given in this immortal chapter of 39 verses as to why 'all things work together for good to them that love God, to them who are the called according to his purpose.'"[40]

Norris also used contemporary events as fodder for his preaching. In a sermon preached during the Korean War titled "The Four Horsemen Are Riding Fast,"[41] Norris made several questionable comments:

> "I do not believe Hitler is dead."

> "Democracies are at an end. Only dictatorships now can survive."

> "If it wouldn't be against the law and we wouldn't get caught I could get ten thousand men to hang every banker in Fort Worth tonight."

> "Now, here's what I look for. Russia has an army that nobody knows—maybe ten million. Russia will strike for the West or

40. J. Frank Norris, "All Things Work Together," *But God—And Other Sermons*, compiled by E. Bryan Clemens (Ft. Worth, Texas: N.T.M. Press, n.d.), 85.
41. Norris, *The Four Horsemen Are Riding Fast* (Plano, Texas: Calvary Baptist Church, no copyright), 5-29.

through the Near East. Russia is going to have that oil in Arabia and of Iran and Iraq. . . . Russia is going to get them."

Cʜᴀʀlᴇs Avᴇʀᴇᴛᴛ Sᴛᴀkᴇly

Charles Averett Stakely was born March 3, 1859, at Madison-ville, Tennessee. The family moved to Montgomery, Alabama, when Charles was a child. His early education and training was in law, but when he was twenty-two, he was called to preach. In 1900, Stakely's "home" church, First Baptist Church of Mont-gomery, called him as pastor. Stakely served the Montgomery church until his death in 1929.

He believed in brevity. Fifteen to twenty-minute sermons were his common practice. His sermons were clear and precise, no doubt reflecting his early training as a lawyer. The few ser-mons available for study were developed textually with a good balance of explanation, application, argumentation, and illus-tration.

Cᴏɴclᴜsiᴏɴ

In the first half of the twentieth century, Southern Baptists reaffirmed emphatically that they wanted no part of liberalism. For the time being, that included a rejection of the so-called So-cial Gospel. Southern Baptists also decided that they were theo-logical conservatives, but they rejected the militancy that often characterized fundamentalism. These testing times called Southern Baptists to re-emphasize doctrinal preaching again.

George W. Truett was an exception in some important ways. Truett's sermon delivery, to be sure, was oratorical. He mastered the posture, the gestures, the facial expressions, and the vocal intonations of the best orators of his day. Truett's sermons were mostly topical, written in simple language, tied to the common, everyday experiences of his congregations, and were strongly evangelistic.

The emphasis on topical/doctrinal discourses preached in for-mal, semi-pedantic style seemed to have left the people hungry for something more deeply involved in Scripture, but presented in a more personable and winsome manner.

CHAPTER 5

EXPANDING RAPIDLY
(1945-1979)

For Americans in general and Southern Baptists in particular, the years 1900-1975 were a series of blessings and conflicts. The first conflicts hit America in the form of World War I, an economic depression, and World War II. Then came a time of blessed peace, although brief, from 1945-50. The Korean War interrupted the calm. Then from 1953 till 1963, Americans experienced another period of relative peace.

There are always tensions. The Korean conflict of 1950-53, the ever-escalating so-called Cold War, the ever-escalating threat of nuclear holocaust, and the Supreme Court's 1954 decision on racial integration were sources of concern for Americans. Nevertheless, the 1950s in many ways seemed an ideal time to be an American. The 1950s seem in retrospect to have been a decade of near perfect peace and contentment for most Americans. The seemingly placid 50s, however, were a seedbed for the near anarchy of the 60s when radical social changes on the international and national level occurred.

In international affairs, the efforts to stem the rapid expansion of Communism, especially in Korea, brought on a near national paranoia. In the early 1950s, a senator from Wisconsin, Joe McCarthy, strongly implied that Communist agents had infiltrated the highest levels of our national government, our school systems, our entertainment industry, and our churches. Anyone who disagreed with or opposed McCarthy was quickly branded as a card-carrying member of the Communist party, a sympathizer, or a moron who could not see the menace of Communism. After a while, McCarthy's witch-hunting tactics exasperated many people who originally supported him. The United States Senate eventually censured him, and *McCarthyism* became a new word in our language.

The "Red menace," however, gave birth to many organizations that touted the American way of life and were dedicated to fighting Communism. Many of these organizations equated their commitment to patriotism to their commitment to Christ.

In 1948, the United Nations sanctioned the re-establishment of the nation Israel. Israel's consistent military victories since 1948 were and are seen by many Southern Baptist preachers as a sign of the nearness of the second coming of Christ. One of the many books written on the re-founding of Israel was a best-seller for several months. Even though the predictions of the book on Israel and the second coming proved erroneous, Southern Baptist preaching on the subject remained intense.

Changes in the American "way of life" were drastic. The changes that most directly affected preaching were growing governmental intervention in our daily lives, the urbanization of America, and the "shrinking" of America by increased mobility and the rise of television.

Before the economic depression that began in 1929, Americans took great pride in their individualism and in their ingenuity. President Franklin Roosevelt mustered all of the resources of the federal government in an attempt to create new jobs. Welfare and other programs (Social Security, for example) were initiated. New and often needed legislation began to be considered in order to extend constitutional guarantees to people who were deprived of their rights in various states. The old principle of the best government is the government that governs least was largely rejected. Many Southern Baptist sermons castigated the encroachment of the federal government in everyday affairs. A re-commitment to the separation of church and state was heavily endorsed from Southern Baptist pulpits.

Perhaps the rapid urbanization of America necessitated increased governmental involvement in the lives of its citizens. Sometime in the late 1960s the population of America passed 200 million. It had taken America about 425 years to pass the 100 million mark (103,414,000 in 1920), and in less than fifty years later, the population had exploded to 203,184,000 according to the 1970 census. In 1940, 31,000,000 Americans lived on farms, and 72,000,000 lived in a city or its suburbs. By 1970 the farm population was reduced to 10,000,000, and the urban population increased to 137,000,000. Southern Baptist preachers increasingly aimed their mission sermons toward establishing mission ministries in the suburbs where the so-called best prospects were moving.

This new mobility brought demands for better roads. The United States highway system which connected major cities was quickly obsolete. A new system of interstate highways was implemented. The old highway system provided roads *to* the cities, the interstate system provided roads *through* the cities. As one preacher pondered: "If I didn't have to buy gasoline or food, I could go from Golden Gate Seminary in San Francisco to Southwestern Seminary in Fort Worth nonstop." Much as the Roman roads paved the way for expansion of the gospel in the first century, so the United States and interstate highways provided a means for Southern Baptists to found churches in every state outside of the South. (The founding of churches in Hawaii is the exception).

Along with this increased mobility came the rise of television. Southern Baptists were quick to understand and use television. At first, they thought that radio and television would be the key to reaching every home in America with the message of Jesus. Southern Baptists' first syndicated radio program, the "Baptist Hour," was broadcast January 5, 1941. Unfortunately, the vast majority of non-Christian Americans declined to listen to or view Christian programs. In foreign countries, evangelistic results from Southern Baptists radio and television programs have been much more encouraging than in the United States.

Recently serious studies were done to measure the impact of television on the psyche of the viewer. Without doubt, television has changed not only the way we receive messages, but the way in which we perceive reality. Between the rise of television on a society-wide level in about 1948 until 1975, many preachers lamented the negative influences of television programming before we had any scientific evidence of this impact.

The Southern Baptist Convention experienced these changes with more immediacy than has generally been thought. Southerners, in general, fiercely touted patriotism and just as fiercely despised Communism; resented the intrusions of "big" government; supported the establishment of Israel; watched their sons and daughters abandon the farm for the city; and found television programming to be a new and powerful medium that referred to the South mainly in sarcastic stereotypes.

The Southern Baptist Convention from 1945 to 1975 found means both to cooperate superbly and to disagree intensely. The cooperative efforts came in major evangelistic campaigns in 1950 and 1951, in the Sunday School enlistment program dubbed "A Million More in '54," and in the "Baptist Jubilee Advance" (1959-64). At the beginning of this period, Southern Baptists still had going for them what Robert A. Baker called, "The centripetal nature of the Southern Baptist Convention which tended to pull all denominational activities into its structure. As a result, whenever a new benevolent movement developed and was operating successfully, the leadership . . . endeavored to incorporate that activity . . . on the theory that what was good for one locality would be good for the whole constituency." Baker concluded, "This concept, with only a few exceptions, is a sound one and undoubtedly has forwarded the work of Christ."[1]

Disagreements arose over two commentaries on Genesis. Professor Ralph Elliott of Midwestern Baptist Theological Seminary

---

1. Robert A. Baker, *The Southern Baptist Convention and Its People* (Nashville: Broadman Press, 1974), 345.

in Kansas City, Missouri, came under fire for his book *The Message of Genesis,* which was perceived by many Southern Baptists as undermining the historical accuracy of Genesis. The 1962 Southern Baptist Convention authorized a committee chaired by then current SBC president, Herschel Hobbs, to prepare *The Baptist Faith and Message* Statement, which was presented and approved at the 1963 meeting in Kansas City.

The second disagreement arose over the first volume of *The Broadman Bible Commentary,* published in October, 1969. The disagreement stemmed from an interpretation of some events recorded in Genesis. After the 1970 convention, meeting in Denver, the Sunday School Board was asked to withdraw the book and have it rewritten by another author.

These were some of the social and theological issues that helped form the context in which we may study some representative sermons from some representative preachers from 1945 to 1975. Despite these issues (or perhaps because of them), most Southern Baptist preaching was devoted to evangelism and missions.

William Franklin Graham, Jr. (1918-)

Billy Graham has achieved unparalleled success. "No other preacher in history has proclaimed the gospel to more persons or seen more lives committed to the Christian faith under his ministry than has William Franklin Graham."[2] As well as holding numerous crusades throughout the world, often attended by hundreds of thousands of people and carried on hundreds of television stations, Graham has also been involved in numerous evangelistic endeavors. He has hosted a weekly radio program, "The Hour of Decision," since 1950. He has operated the Billy Graham Evangelistic Association, produced many Christian movies, written several books, and published the world's largest independently produced Christian magazine.

Graham was born November 7, 1918, to a devout, financially comfortable family in North Carolina. The Grahams were a

---

2. Clyde Fant, William Pinson, *Twenty Centuries of Great Preaching,* vol. 12, (Waco, TX: Word Books Publisher, 1971), 282.

church-going but not particularly religious family until a series of events beginning in 1933 changed their lives. First, Mrs. Graham joined a Bible study class and learned to have a stronger, more personal relationship to God. Mr. Graham suffered a serious injury while working. During his recovery, Mr. Graham committed himself to devoting more time to Bible study and prayer. Then 1934, his senior year in high school, Billy "walked the aisle" and accepted Jesus as his Lord and Savior. His friend, Grady Wilson, also made a profession of faith during that revival. Grady announced that he felt called to preach; however, Billy was uncertain at that time if God was calling him to be a preacher.

Uncertainty gave way to certainty in March 1938, and Billy wrote to his parents that God had definitely called him to preach. His first sermons were preached in a swamp to trees, stumps, and alligators. Once he began preaching to people, he regularly received invitations to preach.

> He began preaching many revivals in the early churches. Most of the churches were Southern Baptist, although Graham himself was then a Presbyterian. In 1938 he was baptized by immersion in Silver Lake near Palatka, by Cecil Underwood, and he became a Baptist. In 1939 he was ordained a Southern Baptist minister.[3]

The final years of preparation for Billy Graham's greatest work were 1940-49. He graduated from Wheaton College in 1943, became pastor of the Western Springs Baptist Church in Chicago, and married Ruth Bell. In 1944, he began working with George Beverly Shea, resigned his pastorate, and began working with "Youth for Christ." He preached an evangelistic crusade in 1949 in Los Angeles. Newspaper publisher William Randolph Hearst was so impressed that he sent a two-word telegram to each of the newspapers he owned to "Puff Graham." Billy Graham then and forevermore was catapulted into national fame.

Graham's philosophy of preaching is tied in neatly and appropriately with his philosophy of the Christian life:

> We, as Christians, have two responsibilities. One to proclaim the Gospel of Jesus Christ as the only answer to man's deepest needs.

3. Ibid, 283.

> Two, to apply as best we can the principles of Christianity to the social conditions around us.[4]

His sermons reflect this philosophy and emphasize both evangelism and ethics. Graham consistently prioritizes evangelism, and he uses some ethical issue as a vehicle to sharpen attention on the need for salvation. No preacher in the history of the Southern Baptist Convention has been as consistent in his methodology as Billy Graham.

Briefly, Billy Graham's sermons follow four steps: (1) there is a problem bothering most of us (the problem may be immorality, family, drug abuse, labor relations, race relations, war, crime, pornography, alcoholism, AIDS, etc.); (2) the real problem behind these social problems is sin; (3) the only way that sin (and ultimately, social problems) can be cured is by faith in Christ as Lord and Savior; and (4) the time to receive Christ is now. This formula, of course, reflects the Christian gospel itself.

Graham's sermons are strong in application, argumentation, and application by illustration. He rarely uses explanation of the text. In fact, the "text" for all of his sermons seems to be John 3:16-17. "Texts" that are announced are usually used to draw attention to the ethical (sin) problem, or to set a theme or mood for the sermon. The main objective of every sermon is for lost people to receive Jesus as Lord and Savior. Illustrations are frequently biblical and always contemporary. Part of his homiletical genius lies in his ability to share a biblical illustration and make it sound like this morning's headline, and to take a contemporary illustration and show its biblical parallel. His reliance upon the Bible gives Graham's sermons uncontested authority. His reliance upon current events prohibits him from becoming boringly predictable.

Graham uses two particular homiletical habits that uniquely identify his sermons. He frequently begins his sermons by noting what he will invite the congregation to do at the end of the sermon. Inevitably this invitation in the introduction cites the need to be saved. This prelude to the invitation is usually incorporated in a prayer. The invitation begins with the phrase, "I

---

4. Billy Graham, *World Aflame* (Garden City, NY: Doubleday, 1965), 187.

want you to get up out of your seats. . . ." This specific, instructive type of invitation is another of Graham's strengths. The listener is told why, when, and how to respond, where to go in response, and what will happen when that response is made. This adverbial approach—why, when, how, where, and what—gives those who respond a sense of peace, security, and confidence. Thus, many of the barriers to a positive response collapse. His clear, specific invitation is one of the keys that open the doors for the many who have responded to the preaching of Billy Graham.

The opening sermon of Graham's 1969 New York City crusade is typical. The title of the sermon was "Come and Know God."[5] He related his text and his sermon to the history, unique culture, and geography of New York.

> Tonight I want you to turn with me to the 17th chapter of the Book of Acts.
>
> In this particular passage we find the Apostle Paul had gone to Athens. He is waiting for his friends to join him, and just as New York City is the communications, the intellectual and the cultural centers–and certainly the financial center–of the United States, so Athens was the cultural and intellectual center of the ancient world. It was the city of Aristotle, Plato, Socrates and Epicurus. Paul had been very busy. He was very tired and needed a rest. But he took a walk through the streets of Athens.
>
> Now the other night, with one of the cameramen from NBC, I took a walk through Times Square. The Bible says that when Paul took a walk through Athens, what he saw stirred him. Paul became very upset, and the Greek word used means that he was provoked. He was irritated. He was challenged. He was angry at what he saw. The Apostle Paul saw the moral corruption and the hundreds of idols in Athens. If we look about New York City today–and the other great cities of America–we see the materialism, the money, the obsession with sex, the pleasure, the leisure, the fashions, the entertainments, the ambition–all that we have made "gods" in our generation.

5. Billy Graham, *The Challenge: Sermons from Madison Square Garden* (New York: Doubleday 1969), 2-3.

Eric Sevareid said the other night on television, "It is not doing us so much good to unravel the nature of the universe unless we can unravel the nature of man."

And that's what the Apostle Paul became convinced of when he saw all that was happening in Athens. And I tell you that when I walk the streets of New York City, and when I walk the streets of the other great metropolitan areas of the western world, I, too, become stirred.

The only explanation of the text in this sermon has already been cited. That is, the historical context of Acts 17, and the reference to the Greek used that described Paul's attitude. First-hand theological assertions are usually general. For example, "The Bible says man is rebellious against God. The Bible says, man is alienated from God. The Bible says man is cut off from God because of sin."[6]

Application and illustration abound in this sermon as they do in all of Graham's sermons. To cite only a few:

Is God personal to you—the mighty God of Creation? When those astronauts were out on the other side of the moon and they were showing pictures of our earth, and we realized there are hundreds and billions of planets and stars out there in space, one of my friends, who is a scientist at one of our universities, wrote me a letter and said, "I don't know how anyone could deny the existence of a supreme Intelligence when all of that is moving in absolute perfect precision and we only know a little bit. We are only touching the fringes of outer space."

And I want to ask the question tonight, have you repented? God demands it! That is a command of God. Nothing else counts in this life or in the life to come unless you have obeyed that one great command, *repent.*

You know there is a top tune now on all of the jukeboxes, "Turn, Turn, Turn." That's repentance. Turn. Turn around. Change. Change your mind. Change your way of living. Change your idea about God. Change your idea about yourself. Change your idea about your neighbor. Turn around. That's repentance.

This past week thousands of American university students went forward to receive their diplomas publicly. I am asking you tonight

6. Ibid, 5.

to come forward publicly to receive Christ. Let Him forgive your sins. Let Him come into your hearts and give you a new life and a new dimension of living and leave here tonight knowing that your name is written in the Book of Life. Leave here knowing that you will never have to face the judgment, knowing that all of your sins are forgiven, knowing that you are going to heaven when you die, with a new power to face the problems and the difficulties that you face in your life. How are we going to do it?

Then comes the invitation:

I am going to ask hundreds of you to get out of your seats all over this great stadium from wherever you are and come and stand in front of this platform. . . .

The subsequent sermons of the crusade included the invitation in the introduction. This introduction to the sermon "Truth and Freedom"[7] is typical:

I'm going to ask that we bow our heads in prayer. Every head bowed and every eye closed. There are many of you here tonight and many watching by television who have a need in your life. You're not quite sure what it is. You've tried to find satisfaction and fulfillment and peace and happiness in a thousand different ways, but you've failed. Tonight you can make the great commitment that can change and transform your entire life. You could commit your life to Christ. And that little simple act of commitment can change the direction you're now going and bring about a whole new situation in your life. You can put your trust and your faith and your confidence in Christ tonight.

Our Father and our God, we thank Thee and praise Thee that at this moment of history we have a Gospel of forgiveness and peace and hope, that we do not despair as other men. We as Christians are not pessimistic. We're optimistic because Christ has been raised from the dead, and we know that righteousness is going to triumph ultimately because of Him. We pray tonight that many in this Garden and those watching by television will be convinced of their need of the Savior and be drawn to Him. For we ask it in His Name. Amen.

Fant and Pinson grasped one of the chief strengths of Graham as a preacher and as a Christian leader.

7. Ibid, 87-102.

> Graham conveys the impression of regarding himself as one with a vitally important, undeniable message from a source of absolute power and authority. He is convinced that the message does not originate with him, nor is the power or authority his. Therefore he is able to speak with confidence and yet humility.
>
> More than any other single factor, this sense of ordained authority explains his charismatic qualities in the face of skeptical, often hostile audiences.[8]

RoberT GreeNe Lee (1886-1978)

To understand Lee's ministry, one must be aware of his fervent desire to be a success, in the eyes of God, in the ministry. While visiting the study of a church in which he was preaching a revival, Lee glanced through a book of sermons. He looked toward his friend, an evangelistic singer named Carlyle Brooks, and said, "Brooks, I am going to apply myself and see if I can't be the best preacher God can make out of a man."[9]

R. G. Lee was born on a farm in South Carolina on November 11, 1886. He was the son of a sharecropper, the fifth of eight children born to David and Sally Lee. He was forced to sacrifice early education for work on the farm. When he gave his life to God at the age of twelve, he was plowing a field.

> He made his way behind the plow handles behind a white mule. . . . Oppressed by a feeling that he needed the help of God, he drove to the end of a row by an old rail fence. There he stopped the mule and left the plow. . . . A young boy got down on his knees, took off his straw hat and started talking to God. "O Lord," he prayed, "if you will save me, I'll do anything you want me to do. I'll even preach, or anything."[10]

Lee was baptized at the Fort Mill Baptist Church in 1898, and he was ordained to the gospel ministry by that church in 1910.

His father was a stern taskmaster who had no patience with idleness or dishonesty. He expected his children to stay busy ev-

---

8. Fant and Pinson, *Twenty Centuries of Great Preachers,* 299-300.
9. John E. Huss, *Robert G. Lee* (Grand Rapids: Zondervan, 1967), 98-99.
10. Ibid., 29.

ery day except Sunday. This early work philosophy was evident throughout Lee's ministry.[11]

Lee served as pastor of several churches. His most notable ministry was at Bellevue Baptist Church, Memphis, Tennessee, 1927-60. Earlier, he was pastor of the First Baptist Church of New Orleans (1922-25) and Citadel Square Baptist Church, Charleston, South Carolina (1925-27). A unique facet of his ministry is that he never preached "a trial sermon."

Despite his lack of early education, Lee graduated from Furman University in 1913 with a Bachelor of Arts. He earned a Doctor of Philosophy from the University of Chicago Law School in 1919. He served as president of the Tennessee Baptist State Convention from 1932 to 1935, and as president of the Southern Baptist Convention from 1949 to 1951. He preached the Southern Baptist Convention sermons in 1930, 1934, and 1938. He was one of the speakers at the Baptist World Alliance meeting in Cleveland in 1950. In his retirement he continued to be active as a preacher and was frequently asked to preach during revival meetings, evangelistic conferences, and denominational functions.

Lee wrote his sermons in longhand. Huss said that Lee did his best thinking as he wrote.

> What is Lee's method of sermonizing? He writes out every work in long hand: for he thinks best with a pen in hand. As his pen glides over the ruled lines on yellow legal paper, he is able to concentrate and create. His first steps are to study carefully his text and then decide on a subject. Often he gives hours of thought to the opening statement in order that it be exactly right. From that point he painstakingly develops his sermons, writing at odd moments all during the day. He is able to write despite frequent interruptions. After Lee has written out his sermon, he gives it to his secretary to be typed. Then he reads his sermon frequently, not to memorize, but to get mental pictures of its content. He preaches extemporaneously.[12]

In a personal interview in October, 1972, Lee outlined his approach to sermon preparation.

---

11. Ibid., 17.
12. Ibid., 144-45.

The first thing every preacher should do is shut himself away in a quiet place to pray. If he is going to preach the Word of God, then he better talk to God first. . . . I pray before I study. . . . I pray while I study. . . .

While I study, I study the Bible. If a preacher is going to preach the Word of God—and he should preach nothing else—he should go to God's Word. . . . Then, I try to think of how I can move lost men. I organize my work with sinners in need of the love of God in mind. I try to preach evangelistically. I don't try to entertain. . . . I try to preach the Word of God in hopes that sinners will be saved. . . . Fourth, I try to find illustrations in any area of life. Illustrations are everywhere and as long as they neither add not subtract anything from the Word of God they are fit to be used in preaching.[13]

When asked how he prepared his sermons, Lee answered:

I never dictate a sermon through a dictaphone or to my secretary. I think best through the point of my pen, and I write all my sermons out with my own hand. I give them to my secretary, who types them. When the sermons are typed, I read them over several times, picturing the words, and deliver the messages—usually without notes. Sometimes, when I have finished, I feel like praying the prayer which Mr. Spurgeon said he sometimes prayed when he had finished preaching: "Lord, thou canst make something out of nothing. Bless my sermon."

And always as I preach I remember my need for the Holy Spirit's help, acknowledging, too, the truth that moonlight ripens no harvest.[14]

Lee said his sermons were prepared with his congregation in mind.

I remind myself that I am to speak *to* people and not just *before* people. Therefore, I seek to make the application of truth personal—as though I were talking face to face in private conversation.[15]

13. A personal interview with R. G. Lee was held on October 30, 1972, in the pastor's study, Calvary Baptist Church, Tulsa, Oklahoma, where Lee was preaching a revival meeting. Hereafter, the interview will be referred to as Lee Interview.

14. H. C. Brown, Jr., *Southern Baptist Preaching* (Nashville: Broadman Press, 1959), 113-14.

15. R. G. Lee, "Christ Above All," in *We Prepare and Preach,* ed. Clarence S. Roddy (Chicago, Moody Press, 1959), 83.

Lee is widely known for both a sermon technique and a particular sermon.

The sermon technique was his peculiar flair for diction. His sermons were often alliterative and always descriptive. He had a great command of vocabulary, and he testified that he consciously set out to be a master of words.

> Bob early recognized the value of words. Having an irresistible urge to become a minister, he wanted to build up a vocabulary. As he became more skilled in the use of words, he developed the habit of trying to use the proper words for each occasion.[16]

Lee used his command of language to paint *word pictures*. An example is found in a sermon he called "Christ Above All" in which he wrote:

> No crystal streams flow so purely from stainless fountains, no beams of light come so unmixed from the sun, no fragrance issues so sweetly from flowers as did the delights from the holy, holy, holy Father's heart in embrace with the thrice-holy Son—in glory they had with each other before this world was.[17]

In a sermon titled "Preaching the Cross," he wrote:

> The diversified, systematic sacrifices of the Jews, like finger posts along the highway of time, pointed worshippers to a sacrificial savior. Significant shadows of redemptive entity still ahead, adumbrations of a substance yet to come, by the blood of a thousand altars, these sacrifices—elemental, preparatory, preliminary, rudimental, introductory—pointed to Christ, the propellant center to which the faith of mankind before and since gravitated.[18]

Alliteration was a favorite device of Lee's. He said it offered a way to communicate God's Word in a way that could be remembered.[19] Even in lengthy outlines, common in his sermons, Lee was not at a loss for words. One of his favorite sermons, "The

---

16. Huss, 33.

17. R. G. Lee, *Christ Above All* (Nashville: Broadman Press, 1963), 9-30.

18. R. G. Lee, *The Must of the Second Birth* (Westwood, N.J.: Fleming H. Revell Co., 1959), 16-17.

19. R. G. Lee Interview.

World's Greatest Love Story,"[20] is an example. The text is John 3:16.

   I. The Principal Person of the World's Greatest Love Story–God

   II. The Pure Passion of the World's Greatest Love Story–so loved

   III. The Perverse People of the World's Greatest Love Story–the world

   IV. The Positive Proof of the World's Greatest Love Story–He gave

   V. The Plain Plan of the World's Greatest Love Story–whosoever believeth

   VI. The Perpetual Promise of the World's Greatest Love Story–shall not perish

   VII. The Priceless Possession of the World's Greatest Love Story– eternal life.

Lee's most popular sermon was "Pay-Day–Someday," from 1 Kings 21. He preached this sermon more than a thousand times.[21] First delivered at a midweek prayer service in February 1919, at First Baptist Church, Edgefield, South Carolina, he preached the sermon in about twenty minutes. Afterward, one of the deacons urged Lee to elaborate and expand the sermon.

The sermon is set in eight scenes. The first seven scenes are related to a portion of the text. The eighth scene is the conclusion of the sermon.

   I. The Real Estate Request–Give me this vineyard

   II. The Pouting Potentate–He came into his house heavy and displeased

   III. The Wicked Wife–And Jezebel his wife

   IV. A Message Meaning Murder–She wrote letters

   V. The Fatal Fast–They proclaimed a fast

   VI. The Visit to the Vineyard–Ahab rose up to go down to the vineyard.

   VII. The Alarming Appearance–The Word of the Lord came to Elijah

   VIII. Pay-Day–Someday.[22]

---

20. Lee, *A Greater Than Solomon* (Nashville: Broadman Press, 1935), 116-34.
21. See Appendix B.
22. R. G. Lee, "Pay-Day—Someday" (Grand Rapids: Zondervan, 1957).

Lee used many illustrations in his sermons. Often his sermons came from the Bible, but as he indicated in the interview cited earlier, he believed that illustrations came from limitless sources:

> After I do much research work in history, in literature, in nature, in philosophy, in science, in biography, in botany, in astronomy, in poetry, and in other realms, I see if there are truths I have found to strengthen and illumine my sermon.[23]

A favorite source of illustrations for Lee was human-interest stories. In the sermon "The Must of the Second Birth"[24] he related:

> I read in "The Gospel Witness" of a little girl with a defect of vision from her birth. Her parents were slow to realize that she could not see many objects which were familiar to others. She was almost grown before an occulist was consulted. He advised and performed an operation, and the child was kept in a dark room for many weeks. One bright and balmy night she stepped out alone upon the lawn. Instantly she rushed back into the house in a glow of excitement. "Oh, come," she cried, "and see what has happened to the sky!" Her parents hurried out with her, but they saw nothing but the glory of the stars—something the child had never seen before. Nothing had happened to the sky, but something had happened to her eyes. So the unregenerate man has the eyes of his understanding darkened in respect to spiritual and saving truth. . . .[25]

Lee often quoted poetry and the words of hymns in his sermons. In his sermon "Linked Lives"[26] Lee preached:

> And if Christianity goes, there is nothing to live for. Byron, in his poem "Darkness," gives us the picture of just what would happen:
>
> The world was void.
> The populous and the powerful was a lump.
> Seasonless, herbless, treeless, manless, lifeless–
> A lump of death—a chaos of hard clay.

---

23. Lee, "Christ Above All," 82-83.
24. Lee, "The Must of the Second Birth," in *The Must of the Second Birth* (Westwood, N. J.: Fleming H. Revell Co., 1959), 52-75.
25. Ibid., 69.
26. Ibid., "Linked Lives," 37-51.

The rivers, lakes, and ocean all stood still,
And nothing stirr'd within their silent depths.

Darkness like doom, will settle upon the modern and spiritual
world if the religion of Jesus should be taken away.[27]

The introductions to most of Lee's sermons were brief, usually an assertion or exposition from the text or context.

Although Lee wove the scriptural text throughout the body of his sermons, he was not primarily an expository preacher. The title of his sermon was often developed rather than the text. Lee developed the thought or thrust of the text rather than simply expounding on the text verse by verse or phrase by phrase. As noted in "The World's Greatest Love Story," each point was attached to a word or phrase in the text. But what was developed in the sermon was the title rather than the verse. Lee was able to preach biblical sermons without slavish adherence to a purely expository method.

Wallie Amos Criswell (1909-)

His mother decided that her son, Wallie Amos Criswell (W.A.) would study medicine and become a physician. His father advised him not to plan on a career in the ministry. W.A., however, claims he never aspired to be anything but a pastor.

I just know that even before I was saved (at age ten), the Lord planted it deep in my heart that I would be a pastor—not an evangelist, not a missionary, but a pastor.[28]

Criswell was born December 19, 1909, in Eldorado, Oklahoma. Five years later, his family moved to Texline, Texas. Family life and church life were almost synonymous with the Criswells. W.A. and his brothers and sisters were trained to study the Bible, pray, and to be Christian stewards. Criswell recalls that his first attempt to read the Bible from Genesis to Revelation came when he was six years old.[29] He also recalls that a housewife in Tex-

---

27. Ibid., 46.
28. W. A. Criswell, *Standing on the Promise: The Autobiography of W. A. Criswell* (Irving, TX: Word), 1990, 26.
29. Ibid, 24-25.

line, who had been an elocution teacher before her marriage, gave him his first lessons in proper public speaking.

Shortly after W.A. completed grade school, the family moved to Amarillo so that the two youngest boys, W. A. and Currie, could graduate from an accredited high school. During those years they served and worshiped at Amarillo's First Baptist Church. With his accredited diploma in hand, W. A. enrolled at Baylor University in 1927. A. J. Armstrong, a professor of English, and Henry Trentham, a professor of Greek, were his favorite teachers.

The Amarillo church ordained him in 1928, and he served several small churches in the Waco area on a part-time basis. He continued to pastor small churches part-time while he was a student at Southern Seminary. While at the seminary, he met his wife Betty, and they were married in 1935. Two years later, he earned the doctor of philosophy degree. His friends affectionately referred to him as the "holy-roller with a Ph.D."

Criswell pastored at First Baptist Church of Chickasha, Oklahoma, from 1937 to 1941; First Baptist Church, Muskogee, Oklahoma, 1941-44; and the First Baptist Church, Dallas, Texas, from 1944 to the present time.[30]

At First Baptist Church of Muskogee he inherited the library of the previous pastor, A. N. Hall. As Criswell read Hall's sermons, he became enraptured with expository preaching.

> Suddenly I found myself really proclaiming the Word, book by book, text by text, cover to cover from Genesis to Revelation. I felt new power. Instead of pacing the floor, stressed and anxious, trying to find some new topic to preach, I was pacing the floor with excitement caught up by the might and majesty of God's Word, eager to get on to the next text, to the next story, to the next book, eager to dig out the truth in every line that God's Spirit presented.[31]

This eagerness to preach from Genesis to Revelation culminated in what must be the ultimate sermon series. Criswell planned to preach on consecutive texts in the Bible until he had preached from Genesis to Revelation. At the outset, he estimat-

---

30. In January, 1991, Criswell's title was changed to senior pastor.
31. Criswell, *Standing*, 158-160.

ed that the series would take two to three years. When the series
ended, more than seventeen years later, Criswell had preached
every text from Genesis to Revelation. With a warm chuckle, he
does admit that some "texts" (for example, in Leviticus) were
"longer" than other texts. Nevertheless, he is satisfied that every
major text in the Bible was thoroughly preached.

Criswell's sermons are primarily expository, and frequently
doctrinal. His early sermons were often apologetic, that is, a defense of sound doctrine. Titles of early sermon books include *Did
Man Just Happen?*, *Why I Preach That the Bible Is Literally
True*, and *In Defense of the Faith*.

Criswell's sermons follow a semi-regular pattern. The introductions of his sermons are typically brief, including the text
and a few sentences related to the theme of the sermon. The
body of the sermon incorporates intense exposition of the text.
Criswell often quotes a Hebrew or Greek word. Not uncommon-
ly, Criswell gives an elementary grammar lesson. In his sermon
"The Command to Be Filled With the Spirit,"[32] he explained
that

> The verb *plerousthe* is in the present tense. "Tense" to us in the
> English language means "time." We cannot say anything in English
> without placing it in some "tense," in some time, as past, present,
> future. But what we call "tense" in Greek verbs in not "tense" at all.
> Greek verbs express kinds of action, as a point (aorist), continuous
> as going on (present), having been completed and remaining com-
> pleted (perfect), etc. This verb *plerousthe*, therefore, being in what
> is called the present tense, refers to enduring, continuous action.
> The translation literally would be, "Be ye being continuously filled
> with the Holy Spirit." The experience is repeated again and again.

Obviously, Criswell's immediate translation of the Greek is
necessary if the congregation is to follow the sermon. From this
scriptural base, he will emphasize particular theological truths
that he has gleaned from the text. Conclusions vary in length.
Lengthier conclusions include the last point of the sermon. Oth-

---

32. W. A. Criswell, *The Holy Spirit in Today's World* (Grand Rapids: Zondervan
1966), 51-58.

erwise, conclusions are quick summaries that transist to invitation. Biblical authority in the sermon is almost always direct.

The sermon, "The Holy Spirit—a Power or a Person,"[33] combines the expository, doctrinal/apologetic approach. The text is John 20:19-23.

> But there are some things that trouble me concerning this position. The first thing is found in the words of our Saviour. Before His Ascension in Luke 24:49-53, our Lord expressly says that the promise of the Father is still in the future. These words were spoken after the meeting of the disciples in John 20:22. They were uttered just before our Lord's Ascension into heaven.

In the Bible book series, the expository emphasis is obvious. Several books of sermons came from the series. The book of sermons on Daniel includes some apologetic. The sermons from other books are expository with strong application to the contemporary congregation. The sermon "Witnesses to Christ" is exceptionally clear, strongly related to the text (which is 1 Peter 1:10-12), and makes strong application to the congregation. The points of the sermon are:

  I.   The Message of the Gospel (is a witness to Christ)
  II. The Blessings of the Gospel
  III. The Language of the Gospel
  IV. Witnesses to the Gospel
  V.   Angels and the Gospel

The conclusion makes strong application and serves as an obvious transition to the invitation.

> But the apostle says the angels crowd around the windows of heaven and look down at us. They are amazed and filled with desire to understand as they see Christ dying for our sins, raised for our justification, and the Spirit of God wooing and convicting the human heart. They are looking down on us, and they are filled with wonder and amazement at what they see. They are like the two angels the cherubim with wings overspread, looking down upon the mercy seat. They gaze at it in awe and reverence. The Bible tells us there is joy in the presence of the angels of God because of one sinner who repents. They look down and are overwhelmed by the grace they see flowing from the wounds of Christ, the salvation that

---

33. Ibid, 51-52.

pours from His heart, the blessedness of His cross and the winning of a soul. What a blessedness! What glory! What a wonderment! And it is ours for the taking![34]

The heavy doses of Greek grammar, of detailed exegetical analysis, of theological assertions built on lengthy but logical arguments have not been criticized as overly pedantic by his congregations. His delivery, though full of pathos, is also conversational at times. He comes across as "a good old boy" who got an education, but deep down is still "a good old boy."

Criswell rarely preached a sermon with casual biblical authority, but when he did he may have been at his best. In 1968, soon after his election as president of the Southern Baptist Convention, Criswell addressed the issue of race relations in the First Baptist Church of Dallas. The title of the sermon is "The Church of the Open Door." The announced text is Rev 3:7-8. After the text is read, Criswell offers an unusual disclaimer: "This message is in no wise, nor in any part, an exposition of the text, or of the passage in God's Word in which the words are found." The body of the sermon begins with a review of reasons why he had not accepted this nomination before 1968. He cited his feeling that God was not in it, his sense of unworthiness, and because of the church. He submitted two factors related to the church—he would have to be gone too much, and because of race. Quickly, he returned to these three reasons as the basis for accepting the presidency: God had so led him, God would equip him, the church could be dedicated enough to overcome problems related to his absence. Then he turned his ample gifts of eloquence to address the issue of race relations in the church.

This oblique approach hardly blunted the emotional, poignant arguments that came next. Excerpts from the sermon will allow the reader to feel the power of the sermon.

> I have been asked . . . how is it there has never been an ugly, racial incident in your church . . . I took it to God . . . and I had an answer to prayer, assurance from heaven that such an ugly incident . . . would never be seen in this congregation.

34. W. A. Criswell, *Expository Sermons on the Epistles of Peter* (Grand Rapids: Zondervan, 1979), 36.

And when the time came that they [Buckner Children's Home] discussed the bringing of their children to the First Baptist Church of Dallas . . . one of the ladies . . . said, "But pastor, some of the children are colored. Maybe we ought not to come." I replied it would be unthinkable.

I cannot describe to you how I feel when I preach the gospel of the Son of God, . . . and then stand there afraid that somebody might respond who has a different pigment from mine. It is as though I were living a denial of the faith, to preach and be afraid that somebody might respond.

(What if there came down the aisle a Buckner child who was colored.) *How would I explain to the child? In ten thousand years* I couldn't explain to that child! I couldn't. But that's not so much the point. How can I explain to God? You tell me how. You give me the words. What do I return to say to God? This child, Lord, out here at the Buckner Home, found Jesus today. What would I say?

This is just the plain, simple unadorned announcement that the First Baptist Church is like the Philadelphian Church of the book of Revelation. It is a church of the open door.[35]

W. A. Criswell has been preaching more than sixty-five years. A person born in 1927 could have been born, raised, saved, educated, launched into a career, married, a parent and a grandparent, and retired all in the span of the preaching tenure of the senior pastor of First Baptist Church, Dallas.

Herschel H. Hobbs (1907-)

Herschel H. Hobbs was born in Talledega Springs, Alabama, in 1907. He graduated from Howard University (presently Samford University) in 1932 with a Bachelor of Arts degree, and from Southern Theological Seminary in 1938, with a Doctor of Theology degree. Churches that he pastored included Calvary Baptist Church, Birmingham, Alabama, 1938-39; Clayton Street Baptist Church, Montgomery, Alabama, 1939-41; Emmanuel Baptist Church, Alexandria, Louisiana, 1941-45; Dauphin Way Baptist Church, Mobile, Alabama, 1945-49; and First Baptist

---

35. W. A. Criswell, *The Church of the Open Door,* audiocassette, First Baptist Church, Dallas, Texas, October 1968.

Church, Oklahoma City, Oklahoma, 1949-72. Hobbs served as president of the Oklahoma Baptist General Convention (1957-58), and of the Southern Baptist Convention (1961-62). He served as chairman of the committee that drafted "The Baptist Faith and Message" in 1963. Hobbs preached the Southern Baptist Convention sermon in 1957 and was "Baptist Hour" preacher for the Southern Baptist Radio and Television Commission (October, 1958 - September, 1970).

Hobbs used a planned program of preaching in preparing his sermons. Advance planning was usually done in six-month blocks. General themes were written out either as topics, texts, or passages of Scripture.[36] Hobbs testified that advance planning also helped him meet the needs of his congregation:

> This way I am able to study the needs of the people in the church and to endeavor to coordinate my messages with those needs. If one just preaches from Sunday to Sunday with no plan ahead, he may find on review, that he has touched on certain needs repeatedly and ignored others altogether. I find, for instance, that even following the church calendar for the year in our Southern Baptist life, many of my themes are already suggested to me. Of course, I am not a slave to this, but, for instance, it is just the natural thing to preach on foreign missions just prior to the Lottie Moon Week of Prayer for Foreign Missions.[37]

Hobbs described his approach to sermon preparation as an assembly-line method.

> I get an idea and put it on the assembly line, and as it moves along I add to it. It may be some illustration that comes out of a daily experience, it may be some new insight into the Scripture that is to be used; but whatever it is, I accumulate these things largely mentally and add them as the sermon moves along in development.[38]

This assembly line began in advance planning.

Selection of a text for a particular sermon was based primarily in meeting the needs of the people. Actual construction began with his reading the passage and then reading commentaries.

36. Brown, *Southern Baptist Preaching,* 97.
37. Hobbs Interview.
38. Ibid.

After the exegetical material was gathered, an outline for the sermon was developed. Then sermonic material on the passage was read to enrich his thinking.

The Bible was central in Hobbs's preparation of sermons. This is evidenced in his study of Scripture in the original languages. Hobbs wrote: "I endeavor to determine the exact meaning of the Scripture involved. This is done through the grammatical historic method."[39]

Hobbs elaborated on this and related his view of the Bible in sermon preparation shortly after his retirement:

> I think that one should begin with the Bible. If he is going to be a Bible-centered preacher, and all of us should be, he should begin with the Scriptures. What did they say to the people to whom they were originally written or spoken; what do they say to us today? Having done this, that is having exegeted the passage, I try to summarize the ideas in the passage that I want to use. Obviously, in the average sermon you can't give a complete exposition of a given passage, especially out of the passage I select those thoughts that I want to magnify in my sermon. In that way one is able to focus on the particular purpose of the sermon as well as to keep it within the limits of the allotted time for delivery. It has been my thought throughout the years that if I could send my people away with one thought firmly fixed in their minds and hearts, then I have succeeded.[40]

Hobbs took a detailed outline into the pulpit with him when he preached. Later in his ministry, as was the case with Truett, Hobbs's outlines became much more succinct.

He is known for his use of alliteration, especially in his early sermons. Hobbs viewed alliteration as a rhetorical device that would help his listeners understand and remember the point he was trying to make.[41] As an example of an earlier sermon with alliteration, consider "Salvation Simply Stated."[42] The text is Ephesians 2:8-10 and the outline is:

    I. Man-made modes of salvation

   II. God-given grace in salvation

---

39. Brown, 97.
40. Hobbs Interview.
41. Ibid.
42. Hobbs, *Cowards or Conquerors* (Philadelphia: Judson Press, 1951), 81-106.

III. The factor of faith in salvation

The Gospel of Suffering," a sermon submitted for publication as one of his favorites also has an alliterative outline. The text is Isaiah 53.

I. The gospel concerning sin

II. The gospel concerning suffering

III. The gospel concerning substitution[43]

The conclusions of Hobbs's sermons most often ended with a challenge, and almost always included an illustration. Frequently, the illustration was a quote from a poem or a portion of a hymn. The last paragraph of a sermon entitled "The Multiple Meaning of Missions" (built on Matt. 28:18-20) rings with a challenge to the church.

> Too long has the world waited. Too great has been the cost of our delay. Too evident have been the consequences of our neglect. The responsibility God has placed upon us is too pressing for us to tarry longer. In faith that our God is all sufficient, in assurance that our Christ has commanded and praised, and in conviction that His gospel is the hope of the world, let us put on the whole armor of God, and march forth to the fray.[44]

Illustrations were prominent in Hobbs's sermons. He confessed that early in his ministry he used books of illustrations but found them not as well suited to his sermons as his personal experiences. The sources of illustrations for Hobbs, as for Lee, were almost unlimited. These illustrations were filed mentally, and he was never known to have used any one illustration in more than one sermon.[45]

Hobbs did not have the commanding voice of Truett, nor the dominating personality of Lee. His delivery, like his sermon content, was based on making the difficult seem easy. Hobbs had a conversational style through which he was able to communicate a deep sense of sincerity. This was achieved by mastering oral interpretation. Hobbs not only knew how to emphasize key words and phrases, but he could give different words varying degrees

---

43. Brown, 98-103.
44. Ibid., 213.
45. Hobbs Interview.

of emphasis. This was a definite asset in communicating his detailed sermons.

J.D. Grey (1906-1983)

J.D. Grey said, "The world is flooded with autobiographies about men who wanted the world to remember them. I just want to be remembered as a humble servant of Jesus Christ."[46] Grey was born in Princeton, Kentucky, in 1906 and grew up in Paducah. He graduated from Union University in 1929 with a bachelor of arts degree. He received a master of theology degree from Southwestern Seminary in 1932. Grey pastored four churches: Vickery Baptist Church, Dallas, 1929-32; Tabernacle Baptist Church, Ennis, Texas, 1931-34; First Baptist Church, Denton, Texas, 1934-37; and First Baptist Church, New Orleans, Louisiana, 1937-72. He served as president of the Louisiana Baptist Convention from 1948 to 1950, and was president of the Southern Baptist Convention from 1951 to 1953.

Grey was a colorful pastor and civic leader in New Orleans. A New Orleans newspaper, *The States-Item*, on April 24, 1972, published a feature story on Grey titled "35 Years of Controversy."[47] The author of the article, Ray Lincoln, said that during those thirty-five years ". . .he has endeared himself to many, enraged others. . .of the city's religious community."[48]

Lincoln offered further insight into understanding Grey when he wrote:

> Dr. Grey, a man who likes to use his deep Southern-toned voice to the fullest, rejects any claim to expertise in the many fields on which he is asked to expound—except preaching the gospel–but that doesn't discourage him from expounding.[49]

Grey admitted that he often took stands on the various social issues facing Louisiana, and New Orleans in particular. He contended that this did not interfere with his role as minister, pas-

---

46. Personal interview with J. D. Grey, October 24, 1972, referred to hereafter as Grey Interview.
47. Ray Lincoln, "35 Years of Controversy," *The States-Item* (April 24, 1972), 23.
48. Ibid., 23.
49. Ibid.

tor, or preacher. He said, "I don't feel I was forsaking my calling, my role as a man of the cloth, by being a good citizen."[50]

Grey served one term as president of the Metropolitan Crime Commission of New Orleans. When hot issues surfaced he guarded against their interfering with his preaching. He said he never "... brought those issues into the pulpit; I didn't constantly keep harping on them. I just preached good Bible sermons, red hot gospel sermons."[51]

Grey's appeal in the pulpit was enhanced by a deep conviction that the preacher must believe in what he is preaching, his deepset conviction that the sermon should feed the congregation from Scripture, and his ability to use humor effectively in the pulpit.[52]

Grey emphasized the importance of the preacher's spiritual preparation. The guidance of the Holy Spirit, he felt, gave him the deep conviction about the urgency of his message. This is a key to understanding Grey's homiletical approach. He testified that he always preached with a firm belief in what he was preaching, and this firm belief came because his sermon preparation was guided by the Holy Spirit.[53]

At another time he wrote:

> The sermon, Scripture, and idea for a sermon must grip the heart of the preacher if he expects it ever to grip the hearts of his listeners. This is axiomatic, and unless these first grip his own soul, he will know it as he tries to preach, and his people will know it also.[54]

Grey has written that he received sermon ideas from various sources. These ideas were filed away as "sermon seeds." The development of the sermon began with selection of a text. The text was studied first in the *Expositor's Greek Testament,* and then in general commentaries. An outline was formulated from notes made during this study and full notes were made from the outline and filed. He took the outlines to the pulpit. Grey familiar-

---

50. Grey Interview.
51. Lincoln, 23.
52. Ibid.
53. Ibid.
54. Brown, *Southern Baptist Preaching,* 75.

ized himself with the outline so as not to be dependent on it while preaching. He testified that this familiarity with his notes aided his eye contact with the congregation.[55]

Grey's sermons were always biblically based, but he did not limit himself to preaching only the central thrust of the text. Grey took a text and then expounded on any other idea that had a close relationship to the text. He did not announce a text and then abandon it in his sermon.

When asked to describe one of his sermons that had direct biblical authority, Grey referred to his sermon "Palm Tree Christian."[56] The text was Psalm 92:12: "The righteous shall flourish like the palm tree: he shall grow like a cedar in Lebanon." The outline of the sermon is:

    I.   The palm flourishes in the desert.

    II.   A palm tree cannot be grafted.

    III.   The palm is an evergreen.

The sermon compares the Christian life with the palm tree.

The introduction to this sermon contains historical background pertaining to the significance of the palm tree in the first century A.D. The opening words of the sermon are in semi-formal oratorical style:

> The lofty, majestic and stately palm tree, the prince of the vegetable kingdom, is the representative tree of Palestine. Through the years it has stood as the symbol of the land of our Lord.[57]

The opening paragraph is followed by historical information about the palm tree:

> In A.D. 70 when Titus conquered Palestine, Vespasian his father, the Roman ruler, had a coin struck commemorating the victory. On one side of the coin was pictured a stately palm tree and underneath it was a Roman soldier standing guard over a Jewish mother and her child. In the Middle Ages multitudes of people went on

---

55. Ibid., 75-76.

56. Unpublished sermon from First Baptist Church of New Orleans, first preached apparently in the middle 1940s.

57. Grey, "Palm Tree Christian," 2. Most of Grey's sermons began this way, and most of Grey's sermons moved into a simpler, conversational style by the time the introduction was completed.

> long pilgrimages to the Holy Land. The name Palmer was given to these pilgrims who journeyed to the land of the Lord.[58]

The first point is representative of the remainder of the sermon.

> In the first place let us notice that the palm flourishes in the desert.

> When we use the word flourish, we choose our word well. We do not say that the palm simply grows, that it merely exists, but we repeat, the palm flourishes in the desert. . . . Beneath the sand is moisture . . . down deep to the sub-soil the palm tree sends its tap root for moisture and for nutriment. . . .

> So must the Christian learn to go deep with God. If he tries to get life and nutriment from the things on the surface he will not be strong; but if he goes deep with God, he, like the palm tree, will flourish.[59]

When asked to describe one of his favorite sermons that did not have direct biblical authority, he referred to "A Christian in Spite of Everything."[60] The text for the message is Philippians 4:22: "All the saints salute you, chiefly they that are of Caesar's household." In this sermon Grey examines the tribulations of maintaining a Christian witness in a difficult place.

The introduction is typical for Grey, with the semiformal opening sentence and some historical background related to the text.

> At the close of Paul's letter to the Philippians he places a bright gem of Christian encouragement in a setting of pure gold. . . .

> These words were written by Paul while he was in prison near the imperial palace in Rome. He wrote this epistle about A.D. 64, during the reign of Nero. . . .

> If a person could be a Christian and live in the palace of this despotically cruel and inhuman ruler, Nero, one could be a Christian anywhere in the world.[61]

58. Ibid., 2.
59. Ibid., 3.
60. Brown, *Southern Baptist Preaching,* 77-82.
61. Ibid., 77-78.

There are two major body points in the sermon:

I. Being a Christian in spite of everything

II. Becoming a Christian in spite of everything

The first point deals with the challenge of living the Christian life in modern society. Grey, in a subdivision of this point, attempted to describe the challenge alliteratively: (1) the Call of the world, (2) Comrades and the crows, (3) Caustic criticisms, (4) Conquests, and (5) Contrary conditions.

Grey was noted (and frequently quoted) for his use of *humor*. For example, Robert Hastings quoted from a speech by Grey to a group of Baptist leaders:

> In a plea for cooperation, Grey told about the rescuer of a drowning woman. He grabbed her by the hair, but her wig came off in the water. Next, he grabbed for her chin, but her dentures fell out. And when he reached for her arm, a cork limb broke off. In desperation he cried, "Look, lady, if I save you, we're going to need a little cooperation around here."[62]

Whether he was formal or informal, oratorical or conversational, Grey felt that every preacher should have a call from God to preach, preach with relevancy but never leave the Bible behind, make sure his heart and soul are under the direction of the Holy Spirit, and believe in the sermon he is preaching.[63]

Theodore F. Adams (1898-1980)

Theodore Adams was born in Palmyra, New York, in 1898. He received the bachelor of arts from Denison University in Granville, Ohio, in 1921, and the bachelor of divinity from Rochester (N.Y.) Theological Seminary in 1924.

Adams pastored several churches, including Cleveland Heights Baptist Church, Cleveland, Ohio (1924-27); Ashland Avenue Baptist Church, Toledo, Ohio (1927-36); and First Baptist Church, Richmond, Virginia (1936-68). During his pastorate at Richmond, Adams served as member of the Foreign Mission Board (1940-50); was president of the Virginia Baptist Children's

62. Ibid.
63. Grey Interview.

Home (1940-51); and served as president of the Baptist World Alliance (1955-60).

Adams planned his sermons a year ahead.[64] This planning was done during the summer months. Included in this planning were possible special series of sermons. The nature of the series varied from doctrinal issues to exposition of a book, or to practical issues that may have needed some Christian application. Adams kept his sermons in monthly folders, and during periods of study he would place material in the appropriate folders.

Detailed planning was done at the beginning of each month. The material in the folder for the month was organized into specific sermons. Special emphasis was placed on organizing material for the following Sunday. In preparation for a specific Sunday, Adams sifted through the material and prepared a tentative outline. Part of the preparation of the outline was an exegetical study of the text and related Scriptures. Appropriate illustrations were added to the rough outline. A smoother outline was then prepared. He took the outline to the pulpit.

Adams testified that a guiding principle in the preparation of the outlines was what he conceived to be the purpose of the sermon. He wrote:

> I find that this helps me to prepare the outline and to keep my objectives in mind. Always, too, there is a prayer for the leading of the Holy Spirit that I may really be God's messenger to my congregation and may give them the Word of Life.[65]

In most of his sermons Adams used at least one illustration for each body point. The types of illustrations he used were numerous, but poetry and human-interest stories were probably used more often than any other type.

Adams's sermons often began with an illustration. In "Making the Most of Life's Inevitables"[66] Adams used three illustrations before reading his text.

64. Brown, *Southern Baptist Preaching,* 11-12.
65. Ibid., 12.
66. Adams, *Making the Most of What Life Brings* (New York: Harper & Bros., 1957), 81-91.

The inevitables of life are certainly more numerous than the proverbial "death and taxes." They are so much a part of life that we are wise if we learn from the old philosopher to co-operate with the inevitable. A popular verse counsels:

> It ain't no use to trouble and complain,
> It's better far to be happy and rejoice,
> When God sorts out the weather and sends rain,
> Rain's my choice.
> A keener insight is expressed in this prayer:
> Give me the courage to change the things that can be changed,
> Patience to endure the things that cannot be changed,
> And wisdom to know the difference.

A friend tells of asking the happiest man he knows to give the secret of his happiness. "In my youth," the man replied, "I was very much in love, but the young lady had a habit of always being late. This threatened to become the bane of my life. At one time she expressed an interest in going to a concert. The tickets cost a good deal, but I said we'd go if she would promise to be ready on time. But, of course, she was late and we missed the first half of the program. She was surprised that I did not get upset. I told her that while waiting I had found a little verse which read:

> Of all the troubles mankind's got,
> Some can be cured and some cannot;
> If there is a cure, find it,
> If not, never mind it.

Those four lines changed my whole attitude toward life."

Jesus found a more profoundly significant secret for meeting life's inevitables. When facing the tragedies of Gethsemane and the cross, he said, "For this cause I came into the world." He accepted the inevitable culmination of his earthly ministry and in Gethsemane prayed, "Father, if thou be willing, remove this cup from me; nevertheless, not my will, but thine, be done."[67]

The outline of this sermon contained five major divisions.

I. You must accept the inevitable when it comes and learn to cooperate with it.

II. Remember that other people have troubles.

III. Learn to let others help you.

---

67. Ibid., 81-82.

IV. Seek a lesson which the inevitable circumstance has to offer.

V. Learn the lesson each experience teaches, and then go on.

Adams's sermon outlines do not fit any particular pattern or mold. In some sermons a given body point may be only one page or one paragraph in length. In the same sermon, another body point may cover several pages. This type of outline division may be unusual, but it seems suitably fitted to Adams's appealing style.

In Adams's sermons there is rarely a strong, direct connection between sermon and text. The idea of the sermon is usually suggested by the text, but it is seldom a direct reflection of the text. Adams's sermons were usually a development of an idea viable with the text, rather than the central thrust of a text. Again, the approach seemed suitably fitted to Adams's ability to communicate with clarity and appeal.

C. Roy ANGEll (1889-1971)

C. Roy Angell was born in Virginia in 1889 and died in Florida in 1971. He pastored Fulton Avenue Baptist Church, Baltimore (1918-24); First Baptist Church of Charlottesville, Virginia (1924-27); First Baptist Church of Baton Rouge, Louisiana (1927-32); First Baptist Church of San Antonio, Texas (1932-36); and Central Baptist Church of Miami, Florida (1936-62).[68]

Angell believed he possessed a unique method of sermon preparation.

> My method of sermon preparation may not be worth a thing to anyone else. Even to me it seems to be unorthodox. Through the years I have read many, many books on how to prepare a sermon and also many statements from the pens of great preachers on their particular methods. Mine is out of style with all of them.[69]

Angell said sermon ideas came to him from many sources, but primarily from stories or incidents which suggested a thought, a theme, or a text. These ideas were collected on paper and put on a clipboard. Prayerful consideration led to the selection of

---

68. Brown, *Southern Baptist Preaching,* 20.
69. Ibid.

two of them for preparation for the following Sunday. Bible references and thoughts related to the sermon idea were jotted down. These thoughts were not systematically organized into an outline, but they were the subject of meditation. An outline was formed later in the week. The outline, however, covered four or five pages. This outline was not carried into the pulpit. He did not write his sermons out in full.

Angell suggested that his use of illustration-sermon was a device to capture and keep congregational attention:

> No matter how full of grand truths your sermon is, if it is not interesting enough to catch and hold the attention of your listeners, it will not do them any good. Many of our preachers are able to do this without the use of illustrations. I envy them, but I have not copied their methods because I have found that to me the best and most effective way is to use a story that the audience will remember and thus nail down the truth more concretely.[70]

His unusual method was well received because his sermons were filled with human interest and biblical principles.

Angell's sermons usually began with an illustration. Occasionally, the introduction included remarks about the text for the sermon. The sermon "The Second Mile" (Matt. 5:41) begins with an assertion: "There is an innocent sounding sentence in the sermon on the mount spoken by Jesus that contains enough dynamite to change the course of the world."[71]

Some background information on the text and a hypothetical illustration based on the text were also included in the introduction. The hypothetical conversation is an attempt to humanize the text.

> I can see them clench their fists until their nails dig into their palms, nudge the man next to them, and shake their heads and look at Jesus in astonishment. Does he mean to say that he approves of the Roman Empire, and that he is teaching that they should obey when they are made to go even one mile? What in the world is the matter with this man? Nothing Christ ever said shocked them so.[72]

---

70. Ibid., 21-22.
71. C. Roy Angell, "The Second Mile," *Iron Shoes* (Nashville: Broadman Press, 1953), 94.
72. Ibid., 96.

The body of the sermon is built on an outline and a series of illustrations. The outline attempts to reflect the benefits of following this teaching of Jesus.

> I. The second mile always leaves a deposit of happiness in the heart of the one who travels it.

There are two illustrations with this point. The first concerns a doctor who testified that he went beyond requirements to insure the safety of his patients. His testimony was that doing the extra effort gave him peace of mind. The second illustration portrays a Jewish boy carrying the pack of a Roman soldier for two miles and returning home, happy and refreshed.

> II. The second mile calls for the best in others.

Only one illustration is attached to this point in the outline. It is a personal illustration concerning a man, whom Angell disliked, doing a series of favors for Angell. This second-mile generosity by the man, Angell testified, led him to adopt the second-mile philosophy for his life:

> That's the first time I ever saw it. But I'll be indebted for a lifetime to the man who lived the second mile for me that first time. . . . And remember when you walk that second mile, you start somebody else down the same beautiful road.[73]

> III. The second mile lightens life's burdens.

The illustration used with this point is an imaginary situation in which a Christian home is brightened by both a husband and wife approaching their marriage with a second-mile philosophy. A clue to the early date of the sermon is possibly offered in the introduction to this illustration: "If you had a visitor in your home, and were going to give him a glass of milk, you wouldn't skim the cream off first."[74]

Had the sermon been preached at a later date, Angell likely would have approached the illustration in a different way or referred back to the day before the milk was homogenized and available for general retail.

> IV. God went the second mile.

73. Ibid., 101.
74. Ibid., 102.

The illustration with this point showed a scene from a passion play at Oberammergau in which Simon of Cyrene volunteered to be crucified in the place of Christ. Angell said the scene taught what God's second mile inspires men to do.

Angell often sermonized his illustrations. The sermon "Diamond Dust"[75] is an excellent example. He chose Romans 8:16-18 as his text.

The inspiration for this sermon came from reading an article by a man who had observed a diamond cutter at work. Much as Jeremiah learned from the potter, the writer of the article and Angell observed the same biblical principle through the work of the diamond cutter. Angell quoted the writer in the introduction:

> As I watched, I realized that he was using this diamond dust to shape and polish those dirty, ugly stones and make them scintillate and glow so they would be fit for a girl's engagement ring. As I stood there looking, suddenly my eyes ceased to focus and a great truth took over my conscious mind. It rang like a bell. God, too, uses diamond dust to polish and shape human lives.[76]

Angell agreed with this observation and developed his sermon on the three ways he felt that God polishes and shapes lives. The points are:

I. God uses the compulsion of circumstances to polish us.

II. God uses hardships for diamond dust.

III. Prayer as diamond dust.

Each of these points, built on an illustration, contained other illustrations. But the theme of diamond dust was held throughout the sermon. The conclusion included a transition from the third point and a restatement of the theme:

> Prayer can be diamond dust. Yes, the diamond dust that God uses to shape us, build us, full many a time is unpleasant. Full many a time it is the unpleasant things of life that bring us into tune and help us to hear what God wants us to hear. Would it not be better to make God's will our will and not wait for God to use his diamond dust on us?[77]

---

75. Ibid., 44-54.
76. Ibid., 45.
77. Ibid., 54.

Angell's sermons were noticeably weak on exposition of Scripture. His style and technique called for major emphasis to be placed on the use of illustration or illustrations. As a result Angell rarely went deeply into a detailed explanation of his text. His approach to explanation was occasionally to offer some background material, but primarily to draw some life principles which he would explain by use of illustrations.

In most of his sermons, Angell sprinkled sentences of application throughout. There is no special, predictable pattern for his use of application in the body of his sermons. The application was simply made when Angell thought it appropriate. Sandwiched between the first and second points of a sermon titled "Same Old World?"[78] lies an example of this type of application: "You reap what you sow. Your sins find you out. You pay for them. In the strangest ways, the payment comes back. We do not have to wait until this life is over."[79]

At other times the application was made on a deeper level. In the sermon "The Second Mile" Angell challenged:

> Now you laugh about it, but oh, the difference it would make in the atmosphere of our homes if the people in them would do a little more than is expected of them, were just a little nicer, just a little kinder, just a little sweeter than anybody had a right to expect them to be. . . . The second mile is just crammed full of blessedness.[80]

Obviously, Angell's ability to tell a story inspired his particular sermon style. At times he was able to combine his storytelling with a strong biblical message. At other times the illustrative material determined the development of the sermon. His style was peculiar to him. To his credit, he was able to preach effectively with it.

---

78. Angell, "Same Old World?" *Shields of Brass* (Nashville: Broadman Press, 1965), 46-54.

79. Ibid., 49-50.

80. Angell, "The Second Mile," 103.

Wallace Bassett (1884-1968)

Wallace Bassett was born in Midella Grove, Missouri, on December 31, 1884,[81] and he died in Dallas, Texas, on October 8, 1968. Bassett was a vigorous, energetic man who did not retire until he was eighty-two years old. Bassett attended William Jewell Academy, Newton Theological Seminary, and Central Baptist Theological Seminary. At the time of his retirement in 1966, he had been pastor of the Cliff Temple Baptist Church in Dallas for forty-eight years.[82] His previous pastorates included First Baptist Church, Sulphur Springs, Texas (1910-15); First Baptist Church, Amarillo, Texas (1915-18).

Bassett served for forty-four years as president of the Baptist Annuity Board, thirty-nine years on the Executive Board of the Baptist General Convention of Texas, and forty-one years on the Baylor University board. He was president of the Baptist General Convention of Texas during 1947-48. He preached the Southern Baptist Convention sermon in 1927.

Bassett collected sermon ideas from many sources, but mainly from his reading.[83] He testified that he spent an average of twenty-five hours a week reading and studying. The sermon ideas were collected in a notebook which he referred to as his "sprout book" looking for sermon ideas for the following week and for a Bible study for the following Wednesday prayer meeting service. Once the sermon ideas were selected, Bassett added other ideas that came to mind. These notes were collected during the week as he continued studying and reading. Later in the week, the notes were given logical order and a sermon outline developed.

---

81. Biographical information gathered from: telephone conversation with pastor's secretary, Cliff Temple Baptist Church, Dallas, Texas, June 15, 1974; Jay L. Skaggs, "Wallace Bassett," *Encyclopedia of Southern Baptist,* ed., Davis Collier Woolley, 3 vols. (Nashville: Broadman Press, 1971), 3:1609-10; and Carl Harris, "Church Leader to Retire," *Dallas Morning News* (March 15, 1965), Section 1, 15.

82. The church was known as the Central Baptist Church until the name was changed to Cliff Temple Baptist Church in 1923.

83. Information for this section garnered from personal conversation with Wallace Bassett in March 1965 in the pastor's study, Cliff Temple Baptist Church, Dallas, Texas.

Bassett said he came to the Dallas church with the conviction that he would spend his life there. Since he anticipated a lengthy ministry, he tried to work out a plan where his sermons, if they were to be repeated, would not be repeated for five years.

Bassett's propensity for extensive reading supplied him with a variety of sources for illustrations in his sermons, but his reading program also equipped him with insights into human behavior. He combined his reading, perception and sensitivity toward others with Bible knowledge in the preparation and delivery of his sermons. He preached in a positive, direct, and almost frank manner. The impact of his approach was felt mainly in the assertions he almost constantly made in his sermons.

In his sermon "The Choice of Faith"[84] Bassett lauds Moses and points to him as an example for Christians who face important decisions.   The text for the sermon is Hebrews 11:24-28.

The sermon began with assertions about Moses and comparisons between Moses and other outstanding men in history:

> Moses is the best illustration in the Bible of the influence of making the wise choice. Our choices are determined by our faith. Greece had her Militiades, Rome had her Caesar, Carthage had her Hannibal, Russia had her Peter the Great, Holland her William the Silent, France had her Napoleon, England had her Wellington, and America had her Washington. Israel had many worthies, but Moses was the greatest of them all. David could sing more sweetly, Isaiah could speak with more sublime imagery, Joshua was a greater soldier, but Moses was the most outstanding character in the Old Testament.[85]

At other times Bassett opened his sermon with the fruits of an exegetical study. In his sermon "The Meaning of Faith,"[86] which was the first in the series on faith, Bassett said:

> The sentence from the tenth chapter in Hebrews which says, "Now the just shall live by faith," is quoted from the book of Habakkuk in the Old Testament. While the New Testament quotes

---

84. Bassett, "The Choice of Faith," *A Star at Midnight* (Nashville: Broadman Press, 1942), 77-83.

85. Ibid., 77.

86. Bassett, "The Meaning of Faith," *A Star at Midnight* (Nashville: Broadman Press, 1942), 20-27.

from the Old Testament 320 times, this is the only verse quoted three times. Two of the quotations are from Paul, and one from the writer of Hebrews. In Romans, Paul uses the term with reference to obtaining eternal life; in Galatians, he uses the term with reference to sustaining eternal life and in Hebrews the writer, whoever he was, uses the term with reference to retaining eternal life. The entire chapter of Hebrews is written to illustrate and amplify these six words from Habakkuk.[87]

Bassett's sermon outlines are not always easy to follow. The major points of his sermons are usually in logical progression, but not necessarily. Often a major body point is really a parenthetical section of the sermon that is not essential to understanding what Bassett was saying.

In his sermon "The Choice of Faith," the body points are:

    I. What Moses gave up

    II. The influence of Moses' mother

    III. Moses' faith functioned in a refusal, a commitment, and in an endurance.

    IV. It was a voluntary choice[88]

Point two consisted of one paragraph. In the context of the rest of the sermon, point two read like a parenthetical statement.

Other sermons did not contain this parenthetical note. Typical of these sermons was "A Star at Midnight."[89] The text, 1 Corinthians 13:7—"Love . . . hopeth all things." The outline of the sermon was:

    I. The Christian hope is life's sustaining power.

    II. Christian hope is life's transforming power.

    III. Christian hope is an engineering power.

    IV. Our great need today is hope.[90]

The last point served as a conclusion to the sermon. Each of the points was balanced relative to length and to the amount of essential information involved.

---

87. Ibid., 20.
88. Bassett, "The Choice of Faith," 77-83.
89. Bassett, "A Star at Midnight," *A Star at Midnight* (Nashville: Broadman Press, 1942), 117-22.
90. Ibid.

Bassett's most powerful sermons are his shortest sermons, which moved quickly from one idea to the next. There is no non-essential material presented. The assertions are strong and easily understood. One such sermon was "What Is Right with the Church."[91] This message opened with a recognition of contemporary criticism of the function of the church in society. Bassett did not try to defend the church against these accusations. He tacitly agreed that there was some substance to the charges. The thrust of the sermon pointed out some positive elements of the church. At the end of the introduction, Bassett asserted: "The church is Christ's successor. Moses had his Joshua; Elijah had his Elisha; Socrates had his Plato; but the only successor Jesus ever had is His church."[92]

There were two points in the body of the sermon.

    I. If the church is right in its relationship with Jesus Christ,

    II. It is right in its relationship to the world and human life.[93]

The conclusion of the sermon pointed out some positive contributions throughout its history.

> The church has led in all worthwhile reforms for the last 19 centuries. With its two hands it grasped feudalism by the neck and choked it to death. It grappled with slavery so that millions were made free. . . .

> It inspired the citizens of this great country to go to the polls and vote out the licensed liquor traffic.[94]

The strongest use of application was usually found in the conclusions of Bassett's sermons. An example, from the conclusion of "The Fear of Faith":

> We have a responsibility as parents. Being a parent means more than providing food and clothing for our children. We cannot give moral and spiritual leadership to our children without setting before them, through faith, an honest example of right living. You have

---

91. This sermon was published in a newspaper. The sermon was clipped from the newspaper and there is no reference to date. The reference to prohibition dates it between 1919 and 1933. A radio log on the reverse side of the clipping narrows the date to the late 1920s or early 1930s.

92. Ibid.

93. Ibid.

94. Ibid.

assumed the responsibility of citizenship. Citizenship is not worth much, no matter how lustily you sing "My Country Tis of Thee," unless you vote your convictions and sentiments at the ballot box. You assumed an individual responsibility as a church member when you joined the church. It means something to connect yourself with the church, which is the bride of Christ. Nothing should be done to besmirch its name. The ordinances are to be observed. In preaching to the world as a church, we have a collective responsibility, yet an obligation rests upon each individual. . . .[95]

Bassett, perhaps, was not a great expositor, but he could apply his Scripture text to a congregation in a lucid and challenging way. His positive approach to preaching and his ability to apply his message account in large part for his success and popularity as a preacher.

PERRY WEbb (1897-1982)

Perry Webb was born in Ozark, Arkansas, in 1897, and spent his early life in Arkansas. He received a bachelor of arts degree from Ouachita Baptist College in 1919, and graduated with a bachelor of theology from Southern Baptist Theological Seminary in 1922. The same year, he accepted a call to pastor First Baptist Church, Malvern, Arkansas. Webb's other pastorates included First Baptist Church, Blytheville, Arkansas (1924-1930); First Baptist Church, Pine Bluff, Arkansas (1930-1937); and First Baptist Church, San Antonio, Texas (1937-1961).

Webb emphasized spiritual preparation in his preaching. He accomplished this, he wrote, through prayer and Bible study. His meditation prepared him to focus his thinking on the spiritual needs of his congregation. Once a need was determined, that need became a sermon subject. The fruit of the Bible study was then added to the fruit of the meditation, and the sermon subject was attached to a text.

His next step was a background study and exegesis of the text. Notes from this study were used to develop a tentative outline. Possible illustrations were noted in appropriate places in the outline.

95. Ibid., 48-49.

Webb preferred to preach without notes; however, he said he did not memorize his sermons, but he familiarized himself with his notes. Notes were not written into a full manuscript, but they were extensive. He filed his notes after he preached the sermon.

Webb summarized his views on preaching and sermon preparation when he wrote, "A preacher should feel that every sermon he delivers is *the* sermon God wants the people to hear for that particular occasion."[96]

A survey of Webb's sermons indicates two major approaches he took in sermon development: (1) The "need" of the congregation often dictated the development of the sermon. His sermon "Doves in the Dust"[97] is an example. (2) The text of the sermon dictated its development on other occasions. The sermon "Virtues of a Wastebasket"[98] is an example. These two approaches typify the preaching of Perry Webb.

The titles of Webb's sermons usually suggest the idea or "need" to be preached. Some examples include "We Have a Hope," "Follow the Leader," "Resurrection Reveries," "Rest for the Restless," and "I Am a Millionaire." As in the sermon development, the titles were sometimes suggested by the need of the congregation and at other times by the text for the sermon. Interestingly, the title "Doves in the Dust" was suggested by the text, but the sermon developed neither the title nor the text. The title "Virtues of a Wastebasket" does not reflect the text. However, the sermon develops the text and used the title throughout the sermon in an illustrative and attention-directing manner.

The announced text for the sermon "Doves in the Dust" was Psalm 68:13: "Though ye have lien among the pots, yet shall ye be as the wings of a dove covered with silver, and her feathers with yellow gold."

The two-point outline is overbalanced in favor of point one. The outline is:

I. Present Condition

---

96. Ibid.,209-11. An attempt was made to interview Webb for this study. He rejected the notion in a correspondence dated March 31, 1972.
97. Webb, *Doves in the Dust* (Nashville: Broadman Press, 1953), 1-9.
98. Ibid., 10-17.

II. Prospect

Point one applied the plight of the Hebrews to the contemporary Christians: "First, here is a description of Christian living, so often sadly true in all its tragic details."[99] This first point was developed in a series of illustrations. Sprinkled between the illustrations were brief paragraphs of exposition. The illustrations and expositions all served to explain the text, but not with direct biblical authority.

Point two was contained in four brief paragraphs. The illustrations and exposition were set forth mostly in an explanatory way in point one; illustrations and some theological conclusions served to apply the message to the congregation in point two.

The sermon "Virtues of a Wastebasket" was built on 1 Peter 2:1-3. The title of this sermon was explained in the introduction. Webb described various gifts he had received from parishioners, including a wastebasket:

> not just an ordinary basket, but one decorated with roses. It has brass legs, and filigree work around the rim. Was this gift a suggestion that I should throw some of my sermons away?
>
> However, there *are* some things we should be done with, that should be thrown away. . . .
>
> Our text is a plea to throw away some things that we may have other and better things.[100]

The text suggested things to be thrown into the wastebasket of life. The sermon was built on the negative qualities mentioned in the text with the admonition that the congregation throw negative qualities into a wastebasket:

> This word malice reminds me of a cat and of its sharp claws. It is the unholy spirit of ill will that seeks to injure others, to get revenge. I am told that in the West Indies it is very common to see the manchineel tree. Its sap is a sort of milky fluid that blisters upon touch, and is very deadly to insect life. Now the venomous character of this tree finds its counterpart in the disposition of some people who delight to cause pain, whose spiteful spirit brings sadness and grief to others.

99. Ibid.
100. Ibid., 11.

Malice: Let's throw it in the wastebasket.[101]

Webb used a wide variety of illustrations from the Bible and from poetry. He made extensive use of illustrations from history, biography, and personal experience. Many of his sermons closed with a poem or one or more verses of a hymn.

Webb's style was, perhaps, more complex than the preaching style of many preachers; however, his preaching was well received in his pastorates and throughout the denomination in revivals, evangelistic meetings, and conventions.

Baker James Cauthen (1909-1985)

For more than one generation of Southern Baptists, Baker James Cauthen and his wife, Eloise, personified foreign missions. Cauthen taught missions courses while working on his Th.D. at Southwestern Baptist Theological Seminary. He served as a missionary to China (1939-45), secretary of the Orient (1946-54), and executive director of the Foreign Mission Board from 1954 until his retirement, in 1979. "In the eyes of many, he is the most important figure in world missions since William Carey. This judgment arises from the fact that he has led in the building of the largest evangelical missionary enterprise in Christian history."[102]

Cauthen was born in San Angelo, Texas, on December 20, 1909. His family moved to Lufkin, Texas, in 1910, and he considered Lufkin to be his hometown. He was precocious and surprisingly aggressive for a child who had a slight physique. In 1915, when the pastor visited his brother, J. B., who was three years older, Baker James interrupted by saying that he was ready to accept Jesus as his Savior, too. The pastor, R. L. Cole, felt that little "Bake" was ready to make a public profession of faith, but his parents discouraged him. They told Bake that salvation was the most serious decision a person could make and they did not want him to make the decision prematurely.

---

101. Ibid., 12.
102. Jesse C. Fletcher, *Baker James Cauthen: A Man For All Times* (Nashville: Broadman Press, 1977), 5.

That night, during a revival preached by Cole, J. B. Cauthen headed down the aisle on the first note of the invitation hymn. His brother "Bake" was right behind him. "Bake" answered all the questions put to him about his profession of faith. In April 1916, J. B. and his little brother "Bake" were baptized.

Cauthen met his wife, Eloise Glass, at Baylor University. Four years later they were married in the chapel at Cowden Hall at Southwestern Seminary. Eloise, who had grown up in North China, the daughter of missionaries, longed to return there, and felt strongly that it was God's will for her to return to China as a missionary. Cauthen, meanwhile, struggled with a growing call to missions. He was highly thought of as pastor, teacher, and preacher. W. T. Conner, renowned professor of theology at Southwestern Seminary, urged him to stay in the pulpit and the classroom instead of becoming a missionary.

The issue was finally resolved for Cauthen in his devotional study of the Bible. One of Cauthen's Bibles had an inscription in the back, which included several passages of Scripture in this order: Matthew 16:25, John 12:24, Mark 8:34, Luke 14:33, Matthew 19:29, Matthew 10:37-38, Philippians 2:5, 8. Beneath the verses was the date November 1, 1938, 10:20 p.m. At that time, he finally knew for certain that God had called him to be a missionary to China. With war raging in China, Baker James, Eloise, and their two children followed the call of God into foreign missions.

Cauthen had a wonderful combination of intelligence, commitment to whatever God called him to do, eloquence, and spiritual humility. Dr. Conner said Cauthen was the only student he had ever had who could challenge him intellectually.[103] Cauthen's sense of commitment was obvious in everything that he did. He prepared to teach his classes, to preach his sermons, and to be an administrator with nothing less than diligence at all times. Early in life he committed himself to always give his best to God.

His gift of eloquence first became apparent in a revival in a country church at Pollock, Texas, in 1927.

---

103. Ibid., 91.

People who had never been moved and who had never been prone to invitations, emotional or rational, immediately came forth. Grown men wept; women were contrite; and youngsters came forward pale and trembling under their conviction.

As Cauthen looks back on it now, he marks that revival as his first recognition of a very special gift for what preachers through the years have called "drawing the net."[104]

This gift was tempered by the most important quality a Christian can have — spiritual humility. A few days before he preached his first sermon as pastor of the large Polytechnic Baptist Church in Fort Worth, Cauthen wrote to his mother:

I'm not blue about going into this new task, but I do feel my tremendous weakness. It makes me quake sometimes as I think of what is ahead of me. It has been a time of searching my own heart. I had to decide whether I would be a John Mark or a Jonah running from a job, or whether I would be like Isaiah and like Andrew and John following the Lord. As never before in my entire life, I am looking to God to help me. I feel, yes, I know that he is going to stand by me. If I didn't believe it, I never would have accepted this call. It is a foregone conclusion that if the Lord does not help me, I am whipped before I begin. Surely God would not let me come to this crucial hour in my experience when I am honestly trying to know his will and then let me be led astray and trampled down into the dirt a crushed, ruined, broken failure for life. No, God is going to go with me. The same one who said, "Go," also said, "And lo, I am with you alway even unto the end." So–I go.

Cauthen kept a preaching notebook in which he listed biblical texts, sermon ideas, special personal and exegetical insights, and sermon outlines. He kept the notebook close at hand always, and he made entries whenever he had some spiritual thought. He prepared sermons from his heavily marked Bible and the notebook.

"Invariably, just the right text and possibly some thoughts on the matter will be there waiting for me–as if God had already anticipated the assignment and had begun getting me ready for it," Cauthen says.

104. Ibid., 31.

On the plane or sitting in the airport or in the car with Eloise driving, Baker thinks through what he wants to say and makes notes. He speaks from an outline on almost any kind of paper. He outlines fully, even extensively, and keeps the outline with him in the pulpit.

Observers feel that Cauthen comes as inspired to the pulpit as any preacher in Southern Baptist life. As he preaches, he is a dynamo of action. He leans into the pulpit with his left hand on one side and his right hand on the other, his left foot forward. He lets his voice carry most of the emphasis, but every now and then he backs away and a stabbing right finger adds emphasis. He does not shout, but his voice gets louder and louder, rising on crescendos. Then it settles again to begin a new round of rising.

"Oh, Southern Baptists!" Cauthen voices that phrase with all the fervor that he has felt in his Master's voice when the latter yearned over Jerusalem. And again and again, Southern Baptists have responded to that cry. "Yonder lies the challenge," he will say. "Yonder on the horizons stands our Master bidding us to follow him."[105]

The theme of "following the Master," especially into missionary work, occurred in most of his sermons. In the sermon "Behold, Your Calling" (from 1 Cor. 1:26-31), Cauthen concluded a revival sermon at Southwestern Seminary with this challenge:

If you're made of the same clay I am, you're likely to find yourself sometimes saying, "What do *I* hear? What *do* I hear? So poorly do I, so miserably do I serve the Lord. So beggarly do I do the thing God would have me do. What *do* I hear?" Yet, wait. "What do I hear?" God chose you, God chose me. . . . I can do nothing else.

"I stand here not by my ambition, not to shout out my own plans and follow them, but God chose me and I stand here as the servant of almighty God." And with it, looking out into this ministry to which God has called you, you sense the tremendous challenge of it; to yield yourself with the fullest abandon to Christ. To say to Him, "only one thing matters, Lord. . . . That I might do that for which Thou hast laid Thy hand upon me." And so living, making certain that you find your place in the will God. That this calling is not a career in which you seek your ambition, but a calling in which you live out the mandate of Christ. Then you live with an

---

105. Ibid., 260-261.

attitude of a perpetual affirmative. When you say in your heart, "Speak, Lord, for thy servant heareth," there is no job so big I wouldn't tackle it. Lord, at Thy command! There is no job so little Lord, I would scorn to do it, at Thy command! There is no place so far, Lord, I wouldn't go, at Thy command! There is no man or woman sunk so low, I wouldn't give my life to reach at Thy command!

Behold, your calling, brethren, in the name of the Lord Jesus Christ.

Characteristically, Cauthen's humility was evident in every paragraph:

So poorly do I . . . serve the Lord. . . . Yet, wait. . . . God chose me.

I stand here not by my ambition. . . . I stand here as the servant of almighty God.

Also his strong commitment: "Yield yourself with the fullest abandon to Christ."
And, of course, his eloquence:

"There is no job so big. . . . so little, no place so far. . . .no man or woman sunk so low."

"Behold thy calling."

Leonard Carlyle Marney (1916-1978)

Leonard Carlyle Marney was a fresh, creative preacher among Southern Baptists. Some described him as a bit of a maverick or renegade. Some said that he marched to the beat of a different drum. These are, at best, insufficient descriptions. Marney had a keen intellect, and his writings are full of insight into Christian behavior. His book *Structures of Prejudice,* published in 1961, is as viable today as it was then. He also wrote in a "user friendly" way long before that term became popular. For example, the opening paragraph of his cleverly titled book *Dangerous Fathers, Problem Mothers, and Terrible Teens:*

I never will be a mathematician. It took me three times to pass high-school algebra; but I do remember what an axiom is. It is a proposition or a principle, based on experience, to which people in general agree. Without being mathematical about it at all, I begin this family discussion with an axiom: *Family training never can rise above family character.* Character is the thing. If it is bad it will always reveal itself, even in the most plush circumstances. If it is good it will always demonstrate itself as good, even in the poorest surroundings. Character is the thing. A family in its training never can rise beyond its character.[106]

Marney was born at Harriman, Tennessee, on July 8, 1916. He graduated from Carson-Newman, and from the Southern Seminary (Th.D., 1946). He pastored in Beaver Dam, Kentucky; Paducah, Kentucky; First Baptist Church, Austin, Texas (1948-58); and Myers Park Baptist Church in Charlotte, North Carolina (1950-67). In 1967, he established Interpreter's House, a study center for laity and clergy at Lake Junaluska, North Carolina. He also served as vice president at-large for the National Council of Churches.

Some of his finest sermons appeared in *The Suffering Servant,* a Holy Week exposition of Isaiah 52:13—53:12. The eighth and last sermon, preached on Easter, exemplified the Marney homiletical touch. The title of the sermon, "Because He Interposed," may be a bit pedantic. The sermon began with typical Marney insight.

> In all the world is there any grace quite like that grace which takes on itself another's guilt? There is, of course, pity–which may be largely a reaction to contrast. There is mercy–the refusal to use an advantage to hurt, or the use of one's resources to help. There is love–which goes to meet a need and shares it. And then, there is *this* grace; the grace that takes on one's self the entire load of the other."[107]

CARL E. BATES (1914-)

Carl Bates believed in thorough study for sermon preparation. He said he prepared thoroughly so that he could dare a

---

106. Carlyle Marney, *Dangerous Fathers, Problem Mothers, and Terrible Teens* (Nashville: Abingdon Press, 1958), 11.
107. Carlyle Marney, *The Suffering Servant: Holy Week Exposition of Isaiah 52:13—53:12* (Nashville: Abingdon Press, 1965), 87.

congregation ever to witness him unprepared to preach. Fortunately, he studied people as well as books when he prepared his sermons. We read that preachers must be more congregation-oriented in their sermon preparation. Carl Bates practiced this for many years.

Born in Arnite County, Mississippi, in 1914, after graduating from Southern Seminary he pastored in Kentucky, Florida, Texas, and North Carolina. He was adjunct professor of preaching at Southern Baptist Seminary after retiring from the pastorate.

His sermon "Heaven and Earth are Shaken" (Heb. 12:25-29) reveals a flair for plain but picturesque use of language:

> I've lived in my lifetime where "winter's bitter chill" was more than poetic metaphor. The trees were stripped; the earth turned to stone; the flowers withered; and the grass faded. The limbs of the cherry tree in our back yard grew brittle and hard. Under pressure they would snap, and the break showed no visible sign of that life-giving elixir from the roots of the tree.
>
> Then weeks turn into months, and the path of the sun shows gradual change. And lo! one day a blossom grows where snow lately had lain. How did it come? I hear the answer: "I shake the earth." Other blossoms come, and the tree looks like a boutonniere for some giant lapel. How sweet their fragrance! How delicately divine each petal! My heart literally sings within me, and some strange memory reminds me of life's lost paradise. The day closes, and night winds blow. The bough is shaken, and the ground beneath is spread with dead blossoms. My tree is bare. But wait! In embryo I see the fruit that is to be. Nothing is lost save that which must go. I stand again some weeks later under this same tree, and before my eyes I see a banquet spread. It is the way of God. "I shake the earth."[108]
>
> Every shaking of any earthly kingdom but moves us closer to the time of Christ. Empires wax and wane, but towering over them all we see the figure of the eternal Son of God. The mob at his feet may rage. They may gamble again for the remains of his kingdom. They may go home and forget that he ever lived. But that Man on the Cross will yet haunt them down a thousand million years of self-disgust.[109]

108. Ibid.
109. Ibid.

Bates supported his content with a deep, warm voice and personality.

Robert Ernest Naylor (1909-)

Robert Ernest Naylor loved expository preaching. This was reflected in his sermons. A master of the simple, declarative sentence, he said in one sentence what most preachers would say in paragraphs.

Naylor was born in Oklahoma in 1909. He graduated from Southwestern Baptist Theological Seminary in 1932. The next twenty years he spent pastoring First Baptist churches: Nashville, Arkansas (1932-35); Malvern, Arkansas (1935-37); Arkadelphia, Arkansas (1937-44); Enid, Oklahoma (1944-47); and Columbia, South Carolina (1947-52). Naylor pastored the Travis Avenue Baptist Church in Fort Worth, Texas, 1952-58. From 1958 to 78 he served as president of Southwestern Baptist Theological Seminary.

His sermon "Babes in Christ" was based on two passages of Scripture: 1 Cor. 3:1-8, and 1 Peter 2:1-3. Note the simple, profound, brief declarative sentences in the following excerpts:

> To be a person you must have physical conception and physical birth. There is no possibility of identity, individuality, and personality aside from physical birth. To be physically born is to be introduced into a world of which you become a living part.

> To be a Christian you must have a spiritual birth. You must be born to a spiritual identity. You must come to a situation in which, as a newborn child of God, you are a member of the family of God. Spiritual birth is into the divine family.[110]

> Paul indicated that the many problems of the Corinthian church were due to the fact that the membership in the church was made up largely of babes in Christ. In effect, he said, you have been trying to treat yourselves like adults; you have been trying to eat adult food. You are simply not ready for that kind of diet. Being babes in Christ has resulted for you in many divisions. Strife, envyings, and such like are common in your church. These divisions had become

---

110. H. C. Brown, Jr. *Southern Baptist Preaching* (Nashville: Broadman Press, 1959), 152.

so public and so apparent that word had come to Paul concerning them, and he immediately wrote this letter and said that the Corinthian Christians were babes in Christ, needing the milk of the Word.

Peter, on the other hand, was writing to a group of people that had been scattered abroad by persecution. He called them children of the dispersion. Most of them were adults physically, mature physically in the experience of living. They were mature emotionally, perhaps. They were babes in Christ, and what a formidable list of sins was laid at their door because they failed to recognize the basic fact in Christian experience.[111]

What is this food for Christian babes? Peter says, "Desire the sincere milk of the Word." Paul said, "I have fed you with milk, and not with meat: for hitherto ye were not able to bear it, neither yet now are ye able." There is no possibility of a Christian life's growing in grace and developing from that of a babe into maturity without the Word of God. One of the first instructions to a new Christian is that they should read the Word of God.

If there were no other reason, this demands that a pulpit ministry be premised upon the Word of God. It is a sad day when the preacher becomes a proclaimer of something else. The Word of God is the guide that is needed in the life of the Christian babe. It is a basic factor in the diet of one who has been born into God's family and seeks to mature as a Christian.[112]

Following a chapel service at Southwestern, a student remarked appreciatively, "When Dr. Naylor preaches, you don't have to ask how he feels. He tells it straight!"

Duke K. McCall (1914-)

Duke K. McCall was born in Meridian, Mississippi, in 1914. He had the rare distinction of serving as president of two Southern Baptist seminaries: New Orleans Baptist Theological Seminary, 1943-46, and Southern Baptist Theological Seminary, 1951-1980. Before entering administrative service, McCall served as pastor of the Broadway Baptist Church in Louisville, Kentucky,

111. Ibid., 153-4.
112. Ibid., 157.

1940-43. He also served as executive secretary of the Executive Committee of the Southern Baptist Convention, 1946-51.

McCall used a four-step method in sermon preparation. (1) The idea for a sermon came from reading the Bible or some other book; (2) material related to the idea was collected in a folder set aside for that purpose; (3) the material was organized; and (4) the wording of the sermon was worked out. McCall advised, "Sermons not bathed in prayer and accompanied with much personal soul searching . . . are not worth much."[113] His sermons were at the same time poetic and helpfully assertive. In his "Help from a Broken Heart" (based on Hosea 11:1-9), the poetic portion came in the introduction:

> The personal experience of the prophet Hosea is one of the most painful, pitiful, and poignant stories in all the Bible. Other prophets were ignored, doubted, driven from their homes, and persecuted. Tragedy struck Hosea, however, nearest to his heart—in his home, among his loved ones.
>
> Most of us can stand the stress and strain as long as our loved ones stand by. A mother's hand on the fevered brow of her child brings more peace and courage than the presence of the greatest physician. A wife's radiant "I think you are wonderful" will send a husband back to the battlefield of business life with the strength of ten. An affectionate hug from that same husband will transform a household plagued with dirty dishes, dusty floors, and crying children into a lovely home. The near tears of desperation can be turned into stars in the eyes of most of us by those whom we love and who love us. But, oh, when they fail, when they desert us, no stars can shine in the sky; no joy bells can ring in any steeple. Every song is transposed into a minor key.[114]

McCall's assertiveness also came quickly in the sermon:

> Would to God more ministers in our day could see the wrath of God revealed from heaven against all ungodliness and unrighteousness of men. There is a place for preaching like that. The preaching which has provoked every great revival has been characterized by a presentation of the sovereignty, glory, and righteousness of God over against the sin, iniquity, and rebellion of the hearts of men.[115]

---

113. Brown, *Southern Baptist Preaching*, 123-24.
114. Ibid., 124.
115. Ibid., 125.

Both of these qualities were combined in the conclusion:

> We have been fooling ourselves by trying to solve the problems arising from the weakness of human love in the divorce courts. We have been betraying our trust by committing the tragedies of juvenile delinquency to the officers of the law. We have but probed a festering wound by trying to hurt those we love more than they have hurt us. Where can I find words which would make you stand this hour in the presence of God, feel the throb of his love for you, count the cost of his reclaiming you? That alone will change us and remove those irritating and inconsiderate actions which rub salt into the sores of human relations.
>
> Faith is the answer when human love deserts. Faith in a loving Heavenly Father will save, remake you and me. Faith in the power of God to save, remake our loved ones, will send us out to woo and win them back. At last, God's love will be balm for our broken hearts.[116]

JESSE J. NORTHCUTT (1914-)

Jesse J. Northcutt was born in Haskell, Texas, on June 11, 1914, but grew up in Oklahoma. He pastored in Oklahoma and Texas from 1932-48.

As a professor of preaching at Southwestern Seminary, Northcutt taught preaching to more students than anyone else in the history of Christendom. His teaching career began in 1939 and ended in 1987. From 1948 to 1950, he interrupted his teaching career to serve as pastor of the First Baptist Church of Abilene, Texas, and from 1973 to 1979 he was vice president for academic affairs at Southwestern. He was dean of the School of Theology (1953-73) while maintaining classroom responsibilities.

In 1963, Northcutt co-authored *Steps to the Sermon*. For twenty-five years, this book was the most popular homiletics textbook in Southern Baptist schools. The other authors were H. C. Brown, Jr., and Gordon Clinard, colleagues of Northcutt's in the preaching department at Southwestern.

Northcutt was often described as one of the great exegetes of the pulpit. He was a master at explaining biblical material in an interesting and thought-provoking way. His sermon "A Drama

---

116. Ibid., 129.

in Christian Joy" offers several examples of Northcutt's pulpit strength.

> In the four brief chapters of Paul's letter to the church at Philippi the words "joy" and "rejoice" occur about sixteen or seventeen times. The pervading spirit of the epistle is that of joy. Someone has described the theme of joy in the Philippian letter as the melody of a musical composition. Another has described it as a rushing, happy mountain stream, singing its way to the plains below, now in the shadow and then out again, sometimes disappearing entirely from view and then breaking out again into the sunlight.

> The amazing fact about this joy is that nothing in human circumstances can explain it. Actually, human circumstances were against it. Paul's joy was attained in spite of circumstances. Every Christian, in spite of everything, can be happy in Christ.

> When the curtain rises on scene one, it is a dismal, dreary Monday morning in the city of Rome. The setting is the closely confining four walls of Paul's rented house in Rome. With him is a silent, surly Roman soldier. It is one of those days when one awakens with a sense of depression and finds it easier to count his troubles than to count his blessings. Let's suppose that the apostle experienced such a day.

> Paul had long planned to visit Rome. Tradition says that Paul was guarded, actually in chains, by a Roman soldier day and night. As an imperial prisoner—"I appeal to Caesar"—he was guarded by the imperial guards. They were the best of Roman soldiers. They were native born, received double pay, and were granted special privileges. Their officers had become men of significant political position. But to say that they were the best soldiers of the first century is not to say that they were understanding and sympathetic friends of the Christian apostle. If they were typical, they were surly, violent, gluttonous, drunken, and immoral.

> For a man who loved Christian fellowship, as did the apostle, these were trying and vexing days. It was easy to think if not to say, "Lord, don't you think that you have made a mistake?"

> If Paul on a dismal Monday morning ever permitted himself the doubtful pleasure of such dark thoughts, it would not have been for long. He must have shaken himself and remonstrated, "Now wait a minute, Brother Paul. You know better than all of this. God has been too good to you and the Saviour too real for you to think like

this." Even as he began to think of God's goodness, the sun began to break through the clouds and to shine through his small window, piercing the gloom and driving away the chill. There was growing light and warmth where once there was darkness and gloom.

In Philippians 4:13 the apostle said, "I can do all things through Christ which strengtheneth me." The apostle had discovered in the indwelling Christ a constant and abiding source of strength. When the days grew long and the companionship intolerable, Christ was a real and infilling presence. When his heart was tempted to falter and when resolution wavered, the infilling strength of Christ sustained him. When one believes in and knows in experience the presence of Christ and quietly rests himself upon the surety of this presence, there is strength for every test and trial.[117]

C. Oscar Johnson (1886-1965)

Johnson was a unique man and an effective preacher. He had the distinction of being elected a vice president of the Southern Baptist Convention in 1948 and president of the American Baptist Convention 1932-33. He graduated from Carson-Newman College and Southwestern Baptist Theological Seminary. He pastored churches in California, Kentucky, Washington, and Missouri. His last pastorate, Third Baptist Church of St. Louis, Missouri, was dually aligned with both the Southern and American Baptist conventions. In 1958, he accepted a professorship at Berkeley Baptist University.

Johnson urged that sermon preparation be bathed in prayer. He summarized his sermon preparation methodology as plan, study, pray, and deliver. Heavy emphasis was placed on illustrating the sermon. Taking a cue from Spurgeon, he felt that illustrations serve as windows that keep the congregation alert and interested in the sermon. His sermon "A Light in the Valley" contained seven illustrations. The following excerpt is a typical one for Johnson.

A newsboy in Boston, selling his papers, addressed a man, saying "Paper, mister?" Phillips Brooks had just passed by and purchased a

117. H. C. Brown, Jr., *Southwestern Sermons* (Nashville: Broadman Press, 1960), 161-164.

paper from the boy. The man said, "Mighty cold day, isn't it?" The boy said, "Yes, it was until Mr. Brooks came by." A light that God has put in us–the light of the Holy Spirit who is the oil in our lamps, the never-exhausted supply which God gives to light us on our way–burns brightly until the end of the perfect day. Yes, there is a light around us in the person of the Holy Spirit. We need to be assured of His presence today.[118]

Conclusion

Billy Graham was one of the first preachers to notice that the old oratorical style was losing its impact on congregations. He shifted to a more conversational style of preaching and found it widely appealing. R. G. Lee, W. A. Criswell, and Herschel Hobbs were strong oratorical preachers. Lee never changed and probably never saw a need to. He was an immensely popular preacher until the day he died. Criswell maintains a strong oratorical style, but has been able to blend into it a personal and personable conversational approach. Hobbs also became more conversational in his style, especially as he settled into preaching on the "Baptist Hour."

Graham maintains an almost purely topical style of preaching. Criswell and Hobbs, on the other hand, sensed a strong hunger for expository type preaching. Topical preaching remained popular from 1945 to 1979, but a vast majority of preachers, in theory, if not in practice, extolled expository preaching. Congregations seemed deeply interested in biblical details. The practice of relating one Scripture text to another Scripture text to verify a particular biblical interpretation captivated congregations. Biblical word studies and historical context fascinated many congregations. Both topical and expository preaching flourished during this time period. As always, a strong evangelistic emphasis was maintained during this period.

---

118. Brown, *Southern Baptist Preaching,* op. cit., 111.

CHAPTER 6

WHERE ARE WE GOING?

In October 1959, a young Southern Baptist preached his first sermon. As he recalls, his text was "Old Testament, and it took me eight minutes to cover it." He had sensed that the congregation was incredulous when he walked the aisle a few Sundays before and announced that God had called him to preach. After his sermon, he sensed they were certain he was not called of God to preach. He, however, had an opposite reaction. He knew he had probably set a record for the world's poorest sermon. Nevertheless, he also knew that God had indeed called him, and that he was capable of doing a much better job than he had done in his first try at preaching.

He was courageous enough to seek feedback from the congregation. One member, a kindly deacon, said, "you had only one point in your sermon. All Baptist sermons must have *three* points, and it would be helpful if you included a poem." The aspiring preacher responded that he had observed that almost every sermon he had heard in his twenty-two years of life had three points, a poem, and a sob story. "So, I thought I would be different and try to have one point and make it well." The deacon smiled tolerantly and said, "you would do well to remember that Baptist sermons have *always* had three points. From our earliest days, Baptist sermons have never deviated from this pattern. Never strive to be different. Just do it the time proven Baptist way—three points and a bit of poetry." Actually, Baptist sermons are much more flexible than that.

Baptist sermons in the South have had the same basic elements, but each has had its own distinctives. As we have noted, some sermons have been Bible-centered and then related to some current issue. Some sermons were issue-centered and then related to the Bible. Some sermons were doctrinal with a teaching objective. Some sermons were doctrinal with a polemical objective in mind. Some sermons were a defense of a particular doctrine or a particular point of Baptist polity. Numerous sermons were evangelistic. Numerous others were thoroughly supportive of home and foreign missions. It is difficult to say just what Baptist sermons have *always* been, but the similarities and differences in Baptist preaching over the years have been more a matter of substance than of form.

If there has been a constant in Southern Baptist preaching, it would revolve around evangelism and missions. Southern Baptists have always been unapologetically evangelism- and missions-minded. Southern Baptist preachers have reflected and promoted this concern. Southern Baptist evangelistic preaching has always been based on the Lordship of Christ, His atoning death, His bodily resurrection, His power to provide us with a born-again experience, and the hope of His second coming. At no point in the study of Baptist preaching in the South does this evangelism-missions effort appear to be neglected. It was never totally ignored.

Baptist preaching, in the three hundred years included in this study, has always stood for separation of church and state. Those early Baptists, arriving at "Charles Town" from England and France, staked their lives on the right to worship freely God without interference from any government. From John Leland in the eighteenth century to W. A. Criswell in the twentieth century, this has been another constant in Southern Baptist preaching. Leland, preaching against the support for churches, challenged anyone to document Scriptural support for such a tax. Criswell, preaching in 1968 against tax support of churches, said, "I have said a thousand times with regard to tax money for church institutions, I have said this sentence, 'You cannot separate a church from its institutions, and to give tax support to an institution owned and operated by the church is to give tax support to the church itself?"[1] Baptist preaching has stood constantly for separation of church and state.

At times Southern Baptist preaching centered on the Bible and made some application to those who listened. At other times Southern Baptist preaching centered on some pertinent issue in the lives of those who listened and related the issue to the Bible. There is no easy way to chart these differences. Bible-centered preaching and issue-centered preaching often occurred in the same era. While Oliver Hart preached on religious freedom and supported the Revolutionary War, the preaching of Shubal Stearns and Daniel Marshall heavily emphasized evangelism. Both kinds of preaching were done by the same preachers. Some testimonies on the preaching of Stearns and Marshall tell us that they supported the cause of religious freedom in some of their sermons. Southern Baptist preaching historically has sought at times to bring the Bible to bear on the challenges and problems of everyday life. At other times, the challenges and problems of everyday life were brought to bear on the Bible. The important thing for us to note is that Southern Baptist preaching, at its best, has sought to bring together the eternal word of God to a contemporary congregation in a meaningful way.

In order to bridge this communications gap—bringing a contemporary word from an ancient document—Southern Baptist preachers, at their best, have learned to do thorough preparation. If there is a common denominator among the most able preachers, it is that they dedicated themselves to hard work in their sermon preparations. Early in his preaching career, R.G. Lee looked up from his Bible and turned to his dear friend Carlyle Brooks and said, "Carlyle, I am going to dedicate myself to God to see if he can make me the best preacher that I can be." This kind of dedication took our best preachers to their knees in prayer, to the Bible in study, and to the people in service. These three ingredients—intense prayer, intense study, and devout service to people—are essential for God to make the best

---

1. W. A. Criswell, "Church of the Open Door," 1968.

preacher He can out of anyone. Southern Baptist preachers, at their best, were not afraid of hard work.

These preachers—with a Bible in their hands—for good or ill, set the tone, and, in some cases, the standard for those who follow them as Southern Baptist preachers.

WHERE IS SOUTHERN BAPTIST PREACHING GOING?

So far we have studied where Southern Baptist preaching has been. We need to ponder a moment where Southern Baptist preaching is going. No doubt, Southern Baptist preaching will continue an emphasis on evangelism and missions. So long as the Great Commission remains in effect, we are mandated of God to preach with a view to winning the world to Jesus. Southern Baptist preaching must continue to be biblically based and applied to life. Christian preaching is no longer preaching if it lacks either biblical authority or application to a contemporary congregation. Southern Baptist preachers must continue to work hard at being prayerful students of the Word and maintain contact with people. As Truett once told his family physician, "Some people think Truett is brilliant. That is not so. I must work hard to feed the people." The truth of Truett's statement is an abiding one. Southern Baptist preachers must be committed to hard work in order to feed the people.

A SHIFT BACK TO CONGREGATIONAL ORIENTATION

One significant change since 1979 has been the shift back to congregational orientation. For many years preachers were deeply "source oriented." Priority was given to what was *said*, and secondary consideration to how the message was *received*. Preachers must be more "receptor-oriented." No longer can preachers expect to regale a congregation simply by clever alliteration delivered in ministerial intonations. They must understand how and why congregations receive communications stimuli. They need to know why congregations respond positively or negatively and adjust their communication skills accordingly.

The term "user friendly" is also applied to preaching. The term may be contemporary, but the concept is ancient. The first "user-friendly" preacher was Jesus. He, of course, was a master communicator. His opening lines focused the listener's attention on the subject of His "sermon." His messages were always in a familiar frame of reference. Everyone who listened could literally see what He said: "A certain man had two sons." "A sower went out to sow." "In my Father's house are many mansions." "I am the true vine." "I am the good shepherd."

Where is Southern Baptist preaching going? We are much more multiethnic and multiracial these days. Southern Baptists have been trying to reach the world for Jesus for a century and a half. It is not surprising to find ethnic congregations in the Southern Baptist Convention. This is especially true, for example, in the Greater New York Metropolitan Baptist Association, where more than two dozen different Southern Baptist ethnic groups worship in individual churches. Also, a few of our state conventions have elected Black and Hispanic persons as president of their conventions. Our multiethnic and multiracial congregations are served by wonderful preachers and pastors. The next chapter in the history of Southern Baptist preaching will include many of their names.

Where is Southern Baptist preaching going? We are returning to an emphasis on congregational orientation which is described as "user-friendly" preaching. Southern Baptist preaching, then, is headed back to where it should always be—a profound word from the Bible presented in an easily understood way.

Selected Bibliography

Books

Adams, Theodore F. *Making the Most of What Life Brings.* New York: Harper & Bros., 1957.

Angell, C. Roy. *Shields of Brass.* Nashville: Broadman Press, 1965.

_____. *Iron Shoes.* Nashville: Broadman Press, 1953.

Bailey, James Davis. *Reverends Philip Mulkey and James Fowler: The Story of the First Baptist Church Planted in Upper South Carolina.* no publication date.

Baker, Robert A. *The Southern Baptist Convention and Its People.* Nashville: Broadman Press, 1972.

Barnes, W. W. *The Southern Baptist Convention 1844-1953.* Nashville: Broadman Press, 1954.

Bassett, Wallace. *A Star at Midnight.* Nashville: Broadman Press, 1942.

Boyce, James P. *Life and Death the Christian's Portion.* New York: Sheldon & Co., 1869.

Broadus, John A. *A Treatise on the Preparation and Delivery of Sermons.* Ed. E. C. Dargan. New York: George H. Doran Co., 1898.

_____. *Sermons and Addresses.* Nashville: The Sunday School Board of the Southern Baptist Convention, 1886.

Brown, H. C. Jr., *Southern Baptist Preaching.* Nashville: Broadman Press, 1959.

_____. *Southwestern Sermons.* Nashville: Broadman Press, 1960.

Burleson, Georgia J., ed. *The Life and Writings of Rufus C. Burleson.* Published by Georgia J. Burleson, 1901.

Carpenter, Joel A., ed. *The Early Billy Graham: Sermon & Revival Accounts.* New York: Garland Publishing Inc., 1988.

Carroll, B. H. *Saved to Serve.* Ed. J. B. Cranfill. Dallas: Helms Printing Co., 1941.

____. *The Day of the Lord.* Ed. J. B. Cranfill. Nashville: Broadman Press, 1936.

Carroll, J. M. *A History of Texas Baptists.* Dallas: Baptist Standard Publishing Co., 1923.

Cash, W. B. *The Mind of the South.* New York: Doubleday, 1954.

Cook, Harvey T. *A Biography of Richard Furman.* Greenville: Baptist Courier Job Rooms, 1913.

Cranfill, J. B., ed. *Jesus the Christ.* Nashville: Baird-Ward Press, 1937.

Criswell, W. A. Expository Sermons on the Epistles of Peter. Grand Rapids: Zondervan Press, 1979.

_____. *Standing on the Promise: The Autobiography of W. A. Criswell.* Irving, Tex: Word Publishing Co., 1990.

____. *The Church of the Open Door,* audio cassette. Dallas, Tex: First Baptist Church, 1968.

____. *The Holy Spirit in Today's World.* Grand Rapids: Zondervan Press, 1966.

Dargan, E. C. *A History of Preaching.* Vol. 1. New York: A. C. Armstrong & Son, 1906; Vol. 2. New York: Geroge H. Doran & Co., 1912.

_____. *The Changeless Christ.* Chicago: Fleming H. Revell Co., 1918.

Dodd, M. E. *The Christ Whom We Worship.* Shreveport: Journal Publishing Co., 1930.

Elton, Romeo, ed. *The Literary Remains of the Rev. Jonathan Maxcy.* New York: A.V. Blake, 1844.

Fant, Clyde and Pinson, William. *Twenty Centuries of Great Preaching.* Waco, Tex.: Word Books Publisher, 1971.

Fleming, Robert, ed. *Georgia Baptist Pulpit,* Vol. I. Richmond: H.K. Ellyson, 1847.

Fletcher, Jesse C. *Baker James Cauthen: A Man for All Times.* Nashville: Broadman Press, 1977.

Fuller, Richard. *The Cross.* Philadelphia: American Baptist Publication Society, 1841.

Furman, Richard. *America's Deliverance and Duty.* Charleston: W. P. Young, 1802.

____. *Exposition of the Views of Baptist Relative to the Coloured Population of the United States.* Reprinted in *Richard Furman: Life and Legacy.* By James A. Rogers. Macon, Ga.: Mercer University Press, 1985.

Gambrell, J. B. *Ten Years in Texas.* Dallas: Baptist Standard, 1909.

Graham, Billy. *World Aflame.* Garden City, N. Y.: Doubleday & Co., 1965.

____. *The Challenge: Sermons from Madison Square Garden.* New York: Doubleday & Co., 1969.

Graves, J. R. *Satan Dethroned and Other Sermons by J. R. Graves.* Ed. O. L. Hailey. Chicago: Fleming H. Revell Co., 1929.

Hatcher, William E. *John Jasper: The Unmatched Negro Philosopher and Preacher.* Chicago: Fleming H. Revell Co., 1908.

Hawthorne, J. B. *An Unshaken Trust and Other Sermons.* Philadelphia: American Baptist Publication Society, 1899.

Hobbs, Herschel. *Cowards or Conquerors.* Philadelphia: Judson Press, 1951.

Huss, John E. *Robert G. Lee.* Grand Rapids, Mich: Zondervan Publishing House, 1967.

Ireland, James. *The Life of the Rev. James Ireland.* Winchester, Va.: J. Foster, 1819.

James, Powhatan W. *George W. Truett.* Nashville: Broadman Press, 1939.

Jeter, J. B. *The Recollection of a Long Life.* Richmond: The Religious Herald Co., 1891.

Johnson, Paul. *The Birth of the Modern.* New York: Harper Collins Publishers, 1991.

Johnson, William B. *Love Characteristic of the Deity.* Charleston, S.C.: W. Riley, 1823.

Jones, Carter H. *Prophetic Patriotism.* Nashville: Broadman Press, 1941.

Landrum, W. W. *Settled in the Sanctuary.* Nashville: Sunday School Board of the Southern Baptist Convention, 1925.

Lee, R. G. *A Greater Than Solomon.* Nashville: Broadman Press, 1935.

____. *Christ Above All.* Nashville: Broadman Press, 1963.

____. *Pay-Day—Someday.* Grand Rapid: Zondervan Press, 1957.

____. *The Must of the Second Birth.* Westwood, N.J.: Fleming H. Revell Co., 1959.

Leland, John. *Blow at the Root.* New London: Joseph D. Huntington, 1801.

Love, J. F., ed. *The Southern Baptist Pulpit.* Philadelphia: American Baptist Publication Society, 1895.

Marney, Carlyle. *Dangerous Fathers, Problem Mothers, and Terrible Teens.* Nashville: Abingdon Press, 1958.

____. *The Suffering Servant: Holy Week Exposition of Isaiah 52:13-53:12.* Nashville: Abingdon Press, 1965.

McBeth, Leon. *The Baptist Heritage: Four Centuries of Baptist Witness.* Nashville: Broadman Press, 1987.

____. *The First Baptist Church of Dallas: Centennial History (1869-1968).* Grand Rapids: Zondervan Publishing House, 1968.

____. *A Sourcebook for Baptist Heritage.* Nashville: Broadman Press, 1990.

Melton, W. W. *The Christian Heritage.* New York City: The American Press, 1959.

Mullins, E. Y. *Baptist and Reflector.* August 24, 1911.

Norris, J. Frank. *But God—and Other Sermons.* Fort Worth, Tex: N.T.M. Press, n.d.

____. *The Four Horsement Are Riding Fast.* Plano, Tex.: Calvary Baptist Church, n.d.

Pendleton, J. M. *Short Sermons on Important Subjects.* St. Louis: National Baptist Publication Society, 1859.

Pollock, John. *Billy Graham: The Authorized Biography.* New York: McGraw-Hill, 1966.

Ray, Jeff D. *B. H. Carroll.* Nashville: Sunday School Board of the Southern Baptist Convention, 1927.

Robinson, A. T. *Jesus as a Soul Winner.* New York: Fleming H. Revell Co., 1937.

____. *The Passing Torch.* New York: Revell Co., 1934.

Roddy, Clarence S., ed. *We Prepare and Preach.* Chicago: Moody Press, 1959.

Rousséan, Christine McConnell. *The Turquoise Path.* Nashville: Broadman Press, 1943.

Routh, E.C. *Life Story of Dr. J. B. Gambrell.* Oklahoma City: published by author, 1929.

Ryland, Garnett. *The Baptists of Virginia 1699-1926.* Richmond, Va.: Baptist Board of Missions and Education, 1955.

Sampey, John A. *Ten Vital Messages.* Nashville: Broadman Press, 1946.

Scarborough, L. R. *Prepare to Meet God.* New York: George H. Doran Co., 1922.

Sprague, William B. *Annuals of the American Pulpit. VI.* New York: Robert Carter & Bros., 1860.

Stanfield, V. L., ed. *Favorite Sermons of John A. Broadus.* New York: Harper & Bros. Publishers, 1959.

Taylor, James B. *Virginia Baptist Ministers*. I. New York: Sheldon
    & Co., 1860.

Thomas, David. *The Virginian Baptist*. Baltimore: Enoch Story,
    1974.

Thornwell, John H. *The Rights and Duties of Masters*. Charles-
    ton, S.C.: Steampower Press, 1850.

Webb, Perry. *Doves in the Dust*. Nashville: Broadman Press,
    1953.

Wesberry, James P. *The Life and Work of William Screven, Fa-
    ther of Southern Baptists*. Privately printed, 1941.

Woodson, Hortense. *Giant in the Land*. Nashville: Broadman
    Press, 1950.

Annuals, Journals, Periodicals

Annual. Southern Baptist Convention. 1934.

Braden, W.W. *Southern Speech Journal*. Summer 1964.

Burrows, Lansing. *The Tennessee Baptist*. May 24, 1884.

Frost, J. M. *Baptist and Reflector*. February 7, 1895.

Gardner, David M. *Southwestern News*. September 1951.

Hatcher, William E. "Editorial," *The Baptist Argus*. July 11,
    1907.

_____. *Baptist and Reflector*. January 3, 1895.

Lincoln, Ray. *The States-Item*. April 24, 1972.

McConnell, F. C. "The Angels as Students of Christ's Love to
    Men," *Baptist Standard*. December 4, 1902.

McDaniel, George. *Baptist Standard*. May 28, 1914 and June 4,
    1914.

_____. *Religious Herald*. February 2, 1905.

Poteat, E. M. *The Baptist Courier*. October 15, 1903.

Ray, Jeff D. *The Baptist Standard*. March 23, 1905.

Religious Herald. II ns August 22, 1867.

Routh, Porter. *The Baptists Training Union Magazine.* December 1949.

Southern Baptist Convention Annual. 1925.

Tiffany, Henry. *Review and Expositor* XLVIII. April 1951.

Tribble, Harold W. *Review and Expositor* XLIX. April 1952.

Unpublished Materials

Brown, Lavonn D. *A History of Representative Southern Baptist Preaching from the First World War to the Depression, 1914-1929.* Unpublished Th.D. dissertation, Southwestern Baptist Theological Seminary, 1964.

Dawson, J. M. "B. H. Carroll as Interpreter of the Holy Scriptures," *Founders Day Address.* Southwestern Baptist Theological Seminary, March 14, 1952.

Dodd, M. E. "The Radio and Religion," Dodd Collection of prints papers Roberts Library, Fort Worth, Tex.: Southwestern Baptist Theological Seminary, 1934.

Edwards, Morgan. "Materials Toward the History of Baptists in the Province of Virginia." Vol. IV. Unpublished.

Fasol, Al. *A History of Representative Southern Baptist Preaching, 1930-1945.* Unpublished Th.D. dissertation, Southwestern Baptist Theological Seminary, 1975.

Hart, Olvier. *Diary of Rev. Oliver Hart.* Vol. I.

Lacy, Edmond. *A History of Representative Southern Baptist Preaching from 1895 to the First World War.* Unpublished Th.D. dissertation, Southwestern Baptist Theological Seminary, 1960.

Minutes of the North-Carolina Chowan Baptist Association. Elizabeth City: Joseph Beasley, 1808.

Patterson, T. Farrar. *A History of Representative Southern Baptist Preaching from 1845-1895.* Unpublished Th.D. dissertation, Southwestern Baptist Theological Seminary, 1966.

Robinson, Robert J. *The Homiletical Method of Benajah Harvey Carroll.* Unpublished Th.D. dissertation, Southwestern Baptist Theological Seminary, 1956.

Sherman, Cecil E. *A History of Representative Southern Baptist Preaching in the South Before 1845.* Unpublished Th.D. dissertation, Southwestern Baptist Theological Seminary, 1960.

Tucker, Austin. *Monroe Elmon Dodd and His Preaching.* Unpublished Th.D. dissertation, Southwestern Baptist Theological Seminary, 1971.